NEXT PLEASE

(A Judge's Daybook)

NEXT PLEASE

(A Judge's Daybook)

by

PETER MASON

Barry Rose Law Publishers
Chichester

Published by
Barry Rose Law Publishers Limited
Chichester, England

CONTENTS

FOREWORD

The Right Honourable The Lord Woolf
Lord Chief Justice of England and Wales

Our author, Peter Mason, was an outstanding judge. Fortunately the publication of this book makes it clear that, although he is nearer 80 than 70, he still retains the qualities which made him an extraordinarily popular, engaging, and attractive member, first, of the Bar and then of the Bench. He was not the sort of advocate or judge whose name appears regularly in the law reports. This is not because he lacked the intellectual calibre required to resolve knotty legal conundrums. A first with distinction in the history Tripos from Cambridge is irrefutable evidence of this. It is because his legal world was concerned primarily with people, with truth and dishonesty, with innocence and guilt, and above all justice and not arid legal debate. His professional legal world was the world of crime. Though since his retirement, after being for 17 years a presiding senior judge in London's busiest criminal courts, he has interested himself in commercial arbitration.

The world in which Peter worked during the day gave him a magnificent opportunity to observe and reflect on much that is squalid in the society in which we live. To survive an unremitting daily diet of crime not only requires wisdom and a sense of fairness, it is also necessary to have, as Peter does, "the qualities of humility, humour and humanity". These are the qualities that shine through his *Judge's Daybook*. He is not the author of most of the quotations but they are very much his selection. This is why they are such fun. Their selection is also based on a breadth of experience. The toil of a judge performing what was Peter's role does not end when the court rises. It does not end when he has reviewed the day's evidence and made his preparations for the summing-up next day. More often than not, duty then requires attendance at city dinners. Dinners noted, not only for the lavishness of the food and wine, but also for the number and length of the speeches. I suspect that it was his day job that attracted Peter to the statement of Chief Justice Marshall that:

> "the acme of judicial distinction is to look a lawyer in the eyes for two hours and not hear a word he says,"

but it was his evening job which is the explanation for his including in this book a variety of stories extolling brevity and deploring prolixity when making an after-dinner speech.

There are still many judges on the Bench today who would readily acknowledge that they are indebted to Peter for his instruction in the craft of judging. If this book reaches the wide audience it deserves, there will be many more of those who have to endure the ordeal of giving or listening to after dinner speeches who will be equally indebted to the six "tips" which Peter gives. From now on I will certainly do my best to follow his advice. My worry is that *Next Please* will become rapidly the after-dinner speakers' bible and that my colleagues will plagiarise the excellent stories it contains before I can do so! Fortunately nothing will detract from the pleasure this civilised and urbane anthology will give its readers. Having been wise enough to read this book, Peter's readers will have the good luck which he wishes them at the end of his Introduction.

ACKNOWLEDGEMENTS

I am indebted to those who have helped me in my quest for elusive sources, including Christopher Phipps of the London Library, Sarah Dodgson, librarian of the Athenaeum, Professor Dick Hodder, Professor Anthony Appiah and Sir Robert Ricketts, my father-in-law. A word of praise too for Richard Oldfield, of whose skill as a cartoonist I am in awe!

I am indebted also to my friend and publisher, Barry Rose, for his wise counsel and sage advice, and to his proof-readers and to my daughter Pippa Blakemore for detecting slips and errors all of which have now, I hope, been successfully corrected.

Finally I am indebted to my wife Sara for her moral support, for indulging and sustaining me during long hours in front of my computer screen, and for sorting out my many self-inflicted computer problems.

Peter Mason
Autumn 2000

ACKNOWLEDGEMENTS

INTRODUCTION

It was on Bletchley railway station that I first made my mind up to keep a commonplace book. It was a raw day in mid-December and I was a youth of 17 on my way from a northern grammar school to Oxford to try and capture a history scholarship. It was on the station platform that I fell in with another youth of similar age - obviously a competitor - who was patronising enough to give me several tips about the examination, one of which was to garner a store of apt and pithy sayings with which written essays could be embroidered. The idea was new to me, but the thought remained, and matured into a resolution after my written papers were done, and I was invited round to a don's study for a viva. I entered and was asked to sit down. There was then a long pause while the don idly turned the pages of my essay. He then looked directly at me and said "Mr Mason, you don't seem to know very much!"

The lesson went home, and from that time until the end of my career, in a hunt for knowledge, I amassed a collection of one-liners and other sayings which struck me at the time as being witty, memorable, wise, trenchant or arcane. It may even be that they did me some good, as I did rather better at Cambridge than I had done at Oxford, and never encountered a supervisor there who put me down quite so low. And I now confess that my memory for commonplaces was occasionally better than my memory for names; if I was stuck for a name I attributed a saying to a mythical Professor Mowbray, of whom I hoped the examiner had never heard. If there is, or was, a real-time Professor of that name, I hope he did not mind my taking his name in vain.

It is my hope that others will benefit from, or at the very least enjoy, my lifetime collection set out in the following pages. The collection is divided into two sections. The first, which I have entitled "A Look at Life" reflects, as I suppose it is bound to do, my own philosophy of life, bringing together memorable comments on the "still sad music of humanity" and some pert or wacky sayings which made me laugh. The second, entitled "A Look at Law" will perhaps have more appeal for lawyers than for the general reader.

It ends with some actual quotes mostly from Acts of Parliament or from subordinate legislation which illustrate the difficulty facing the parliamentary draftsmen when they try to combine clarity and accuracy. They are to be regarded as Sir Robert Megarry once said "with awe and affection", but I think it is plain that they still have a long way to go. The contents of both sections come from a variety of sources; some I cannot trace; about some I am certain; about others I may be mistaken and for these mistakes I beg indulgence in advance. But I hope that the reader will get from them the pleasure which they have given to me.

These sayings are followed by a much longer collection of humorous stories and one-liners which may be useful to any reader who is called upon to speak after dinner as I have often been. I ought to explain that I had as a boy at school an innate horror of speaking in public, coupled with a burning desire to be able to do it and do it well. I attended the school debating society Saturday after Saturday, and from time to time I would try to speak. But when I rose, my throat shrank, my voice froze and I coloured to the roots of my hair. Try as I might, and desperate as I was to do so, I could never achieve the effortless volubility of the master-in-charge or of other senior boys to whom it seemed to come so naturally.

It was, I suppose, this disability, coupled with an intense desire to hear the sound of my own voice in public which made me decide on a life at the Bar. And having decided to be a barrister, it was imperative from a financial point of view that I conquer any shortcomings which might impair my practice. Whether I succeeded or not is not for me to say, but what is certain is that I had plenty of practice in opening my mouth in public both at the Bar as a junior and a silk, and later, after I was made a circuit judge, on the bench. There is of course a world of difference between a barrister's speech or a judge's summing-up to a jury, on the one hand, and an after-dinner speech on the other. But there is in both cases an equal satisfaction in "performing" well - every public speech is in a sense a performance and every advocate is an actor manqué.

The sources of many of the humorous stories which follow are lost in the mists of time. Many were heard at official or other functions, and recorded on a scribbled note plunged into a coat pocket, and perhaps retrieved days or weeks later when the name of the speaker had faded into oblivion. Many were read in the pages of *The Times, Financial Times, Daily Telegraph, Evening Standard* or other newspapers or magazines, and I acknowledge my debt to these publications and to any other which may unwittingly have helped garnish this collection. I acknowledge also an equal debt to my many friends, too numerous to mention individually, who have over the years relayed to me stories which they found amusing in the hope that I would too. I am grateful to them. I am grateful too to my late father, whose skill as a raconteur was proverbial. At the end of the collection there appears a copy of a letter received by me when sitting as a judge at the Central Criminal Court. A judge receives many letters, usually from aggrieved or disappointed litigants, or (if they have been sent to prison) in darker tone from their friends. But this letter came out of the blue, is a spoof, and made me laugh. Hence its inclusion.

I have, for ease of reference, divided the collection of stories roughly into sections. The first section may be of help to those seeking an introduction to an after-dinner speech, the second, which is understandably by far the longest, puts together stories told by and about lawyers and judges over the years, some of which are no doubt apocryphal, but some are very true. Then, grouped together, are tales about inhabitants of my native county, Yorkshire, followed by inevitable tales about the Welsh and the Scots and the Irish (from whom I am descended) and all they are reputed to get up to. Then sections about politicians, academics, parsons and doctors, women, children and others, including of course those who play golf, (or as in my case, play at golf!) and several other members of society. The remaining stories, shaken not stirred, did not seem to me to fit anywhere and comprise a final melange.

In the belief that many readers will wish to use some of these stories in speaking after dinner, it occurred to me that they might find it helpful if I attempt to write a few words, and give a few tips, about public speaking, in particular after-dinner speaking. I hope it will be understood that such advice is not given in a patronising spirit, but from the heart, by one who has been through the mill.

1. If you are invited to speak, inquire first as to the nature of the occasion and what the speech is expected to be about. It is no use preparing a 10-minute speech full of humour if what is expected is a 40 minute talk to lawyers on the Human Rights Act or to engineers about hydraulics. This once happened to me, and provided a lesson I have never forgotten. Ask too about the time of day and the nature and number of the audience. The only occasion on which I "died" was talking after a lunch unaccompanied by any alcohol, to a group of 20 old age pensioners in East London. I had not been told the age or number of the audience nor the fact that the meal was "dry". An audience of 300 in the Grosvenor House will require a different approach from a group of 15 at a 6.30 pm cocktail party. So, get these matters clear from the start.

2. Also get clear the length of speech which is required, and plan accordingly. Always place your watch on the table in front of you when you rise to speak, and time the speech as if you were a referee on the football field. Do not, as so often happens at City of London livery dinners, go on and on until your audience starts to wilt or leave. If you are speaking after lunch, remember that almost certainly many members of your audience will have work to do during the afternoon, and will be working to a fixed timetable. So, end on the dot of the time suggested by your hosts. If you are speaking after dinner, the timing is usually more flexible. I am often asked what the optimum time for a speech after dinner is. My answer would be no longer than 15 minutes, subject to a small extension if you feel that the applause warrants it.

3. When you know the facts, size and nature of your audience, time of day, type of speech required, get down and plan it. Planning is essential, and always select a theme. A speech should never be a series of funny stories introduced by the phrase "have you heard the one about ....". That would be inelegant in the extreme, and to a sophisticated audience, unacceptable. The theme need not be very profound, but it should be the peg on which hang the stories which you are about to tell, or, put another way, it should decide the points you wish to make and which will be illustrated by your humorous anecdotes. Harold Macmillan used to say that a good speaker tells his audience what he is about to say, what he is saying and what he has said. Having heard the theme three times the audience is likely to remember it. So - decide on your theme.

4. Make notes of what you want to say. If your theme is learned and lengthy, you may wish to write your address out verbatim, but this would be appropriate for a lecture rather than for the sort of speech I have in mind. It may be that you will be confident enough merely to use "trigger notes" - simple headings which will remind you of the points you wish to make or the story you wish to introduce. I find that a 15-minute after-dinner speech can usually be noted on one postcard - either typed or handwritten notes with major points underlined in red. Do not economise on the time spent in preparation - a 15 minute speech may take you an hour or so to prepare, unless you are very experienced and, as in the case of some practised speakers, can do it off the cuff. And there is no harm in practising in front of a mirror or in front of your wife. The one may be more critical than the other. But you must get used to the sound of your own voice.

5. It is vitally important to prepare in advance your opening and closing remarks. Your opening remarks will set the scene, give your audience the right impression as to who you are and where you are coming from, and if they go well, you will have them on your side from then on. For example - "Today is my birthday. I have become a sexagenarian ... with emphasis on the sex" - was

used by a barrister friend. Others may be found in the opening section of the collection which follows. Equally important is the phrase or sentence with which you sign off, remembering that it is necessary to make your audience feel pleased with themselves as well as with you. "Ta very much - and bless you" was a favourite of a clerical friend of mine. Or perhaps use the old Cornish saying "May you live as long as you want to, and may you want to as long as you live!" Or if you are proposing a toast, the toast affords the answer.

6. When you rise to speak, pause for a moment, look around the room, and then begin, and as you speak keep looking around the room. But, unless you are lucky enough to have a microphone, keep your voice up and aim to keep awake the sleepy individual at the far end of the room. If he can't hear you, you are wasting your time. You should also remember that the price of speaking after dinner is to keep off the liquor until after you have spoken. A glass or two of wine will suffice. To forget this commonsense advice is to court disaster.

7. Finally, things sometimes go wrong, the dinner takes longer to serve than had been planned, the early speeches last for hours, the entertainment precedes the speeches and goes on for ever. Always be prepared to cut your speech and to do so with good grace. It happened to me once at a Burns Night dinner which began at 5.30 pm (the invitation card said "5.30 pm for 8.00 pm"!) with traditional wee drams. I was the last speaker on a lengthy list and I was called on to speak at midnight. Half the audience had left, the other half were half asleep. All I said was "It is late. As they say in the Court of Appeal, I agree and have nothing to add", and sat down. It was only then that I helped myself to the whisky.

I wish good luck to my readers and to any who are called upon to speak.

PETER MASON

A LOOK AT LIFE

The man who would be truly happy should not study to enlarge
his estate but to contract his desires
Plato

It's not what you know. It's how long have you known it
Street saying

The paths of glory lead but to the grave
Gray's "Elegy in a Country Churchyard"

Le coeur a ses raisons que la raison ne connait point
Pascal; Pensees

Youth is a blunder; manhood a struggle; old age a regret
Disraeli; "Coningsby" 1844

Old age is the most unexpected of all the things that can happen to
a man
Leon Trotsky

Sero sed serio (late but in earnest)
Motto of the Salisburys, Burghleys and Cecils

The earth is the Lord's and all that therein is; the compass of the
world and they that dwell therein
Psalm xxiv

He comes with western winds, with evening's wandering airs,
With that clear dusk of heaven that brings the thickest stars;
Winds take a pensive tone, and stars a tender fire,
And visions rise and change which kill me with desire
Emily Bronte

1

Suaviter in modo, fortiter in re
(Gentle in manner, resolute in action)
Claudio Acquaviva (1542-1615)

Your tongue shall mock the old and wise,
Your mouth shall fill the world with flame;
I'll write upon the shrinking skies,
The scarlet splendour of your name
W.B. Yeats

Ah! Must Thou char the wood ere Thou canst limn with it?
Francis Thompson: "In No Strange Land"

I sometimes think that I would like
To be the saddle of a bike
John Betjeman

Le bon père de famille est capable de tout
Marcel Proust

Heaven has no rage like love to hatred turned,
Nor hell a fury like a woman scorned
Congreve: "The Mourning Bride"

The life that I have
Is all that I have
And the life that I have is yours.
The love that I have
Of the life that I have
Is yours and yours and yours.
A sleep I shall have,
A rest I shall have,
Yet death will be but a pause,
For the peace of my years

In the long green grass
Will be yours and yours and yours
Leo Marks, SOE cryptographer

To help the old to remember and the young to understand
Gervase Cowell, designer of the SOE memorial plaque, Westminster Abbey

Winnie the Pooh, when asked whether he would like honey or jam, said both
A.A. Milne

La joie de la rue, la douleur de la maison
Madame de Sévigné

I tell thee naught for thy comfort,
Yea, naught for thy desire,
Save that the sky grows darker yet,
And the sea rises higher
G.K. Chesterton

One does not talk about money when wine is on the table

Where the wine is in, the wit is out
Jacob Cats: "Moral Emblems", 1632

Metaphysics is the finding of bad reasons for what we believe on instinct
F.H. Bradley

Idleness is the glory of the sword, and rust its honour
Patrick Purpoole

Il faut vouloir les conséquences de ce qu'on veut

A pedestrian is a man who has successfully parked his car
Street saying

Not all the darkness in the whole wide world can put out the light
of one small candle
Spanish proverb

God bless me and my wife
My son John and his wife
Us four
No more
Ancient Wessex saying

It is a gloomy moment in the history of our country. Not in the
lifetime of most men has there been so much grave and deep
apprehension; never has the future seemed so incalculable as at
this time. The domestic economy situation is in chaos, our currency
is weak throughout the world, prices are so high as to be utterly
impossible. The political cauldron seethes and bubbles with
uncertainty. Russia hangs as usual like a cloud, dark and silent,
upon the horizon. It is a solemn moment. Of our troubles no man
can see the end
*Harper's Weekly October 1857 (quoted in The Evening Standard,
December 19, 1974)*

The world is passing through troubled times; the young people of
today think of nothing but themselves; they have no reverence for
parents or old age; they are impatient of all restraint; they talk as
if they knew everything, and what passes for wisdom with us, is
foolishness with them; and as for the girls, they are foolish and
immodest and unwomanly in speech, behaviour and dress
Peter the Hermit 1274

I lifted the dustbin lid, and looked out
Suggested opening line of a book

Both the men and the women are handsome, but they [the Russians] are a brutal race
Ambrosio Contarini, Venetian Ambassador to Muscovy 1476

The line of life is an irregular diagonal between duty and desire

Never dim December breathed its killing chills upon her head or heart
Lord Shawcross on his late wife

Life has some lousy plots
Humphrey Bogart

Some men see things as they are and say why,
I dream of things that never were and ask why not
Bernard Shaw

Why tell lies when the truth is so misleading?

I cried because I had no shoes until I saw a man who had no feet
Arab proverb

Caelum non animum mutant qui trans marem currunt
(Those who travel have a change of scene but not a change of mind)
Horace; Epistles xi 27

Include me out
Sam Goldwyn (film producer)

Give me chastity and continency, but not yet
St Augustine: Confessions

La tristesse, n'est jamais dans le paysage, mais en soi
(Sadness is never in one's surroundings, but in oneself)
Laurens van der Post

The obvious is what seldom gets said
William Empson

My customers can have any colour of car they like, so long as it's black
Henry Ford

Il y a toujours un qui donne et un qui tend la joue
(Always there is one who kisses and one who proffers a cheek)
French proverb

The secret of failure is to let your ambition outstrip your ability
Harry Carmichael, novelist

Take him and cut him out in little stars,
And he will make the face of heaven so fine
That all the world will be in love with night
And pay no worship to the garish sun
Shakespeare: "Romeo and Juliet"

Cet animal est tres méchant; quand on l'attaque il se défend
(This animal is very wicked; when attacked it defends itself)
French saying

Love and scandal are the best sweeteners of tea
Fielding

Por la calle de después se va a la casa de nunca
(The street of by-and-by leads to the house of never-never)
Spanish proverb

We have doubts whether one atom of useful influence is added to
men in important situations by any colour, quantity or
configuration of cloth or hair
Sydney Smith (1771-1845)

The functions of a Member of Parliament are:
   * to influence his party
   * to influence legislation by his work in Committee
   * to look after his constituents
   * to look after himself
Sir Tom Williams: April 2, 1980

Third parties are like bees; once they have stung, they die
Richard Hofstadter

In this world nothing is certain but death and taxes
Benjamin Franklin

A debauchee is one who has so earnestly pursued pleasure that he
has had the misfortune to overtake it
Devil's Dictionary

Cucullus non facit monachum
(The cowl does not make the monk)
Erasmus

A camel is a horse designed by a committee

If you want to cross the river you must not say unkind things about
the crocodile's mother

You can't do anything about birth or death, so you might as well
enjoy the time in between
Sir Peter Masefield; November 27, 1980

When the Campanile fell down, the elders of Venice insisted that
it should be rebuilt "Com'era, dov'era"

Planning is the substitution of error for chance

Leadership is the power of commanding affection while
communicating energy
Liddell Hart on Marlborough

His grasp of the theories of strategy was excellent, but at heart he
was a shuffler of papers
*Bruce Catton on US General Henry Wager Halleck: "The Civil War",
p.86*

Never complain, never explain
Benjamin Disraeli

Never read a book, Johnnie, and you'll be a rich man
Sir Timothy Shelley to his son (PB Shelley's brother)

Monte Carlo is a sunny place for shady people
Somerset Maugham

The thing about Los Angeles is that it is forty-nine suburbs in
search of a city
American saying

An Englishman, even if he is alone, forms an orderly queue of one
George Mikes: "How to be an Alien"

Oderint dum metuant
(Let them hate provided that they fear)
Caligula's motto, attributed to Tiberius

Can two walk together except they be agreed?
Amos: III.3

My idea of paradise is eating paté de foie gras to the sound of
trumpets
Sydney Smith (1771-1845)

The reputation of a tallow chandler is like the bloom on a peach;
touch it and it is gone for ever
Lord Erskine 1807

Even a stopped clock is right twice a day
Turkish proverb

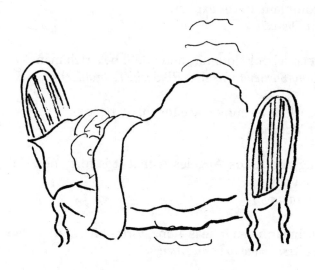

Love doesn't make the world go round. Up and down maybe,
but not around
Anon

When you've left the bridge you shouldn't spit on the deck
Stanley Baldwin

A person who never put a foot wrong never put a foot anywhere
Ernest Bevin

For good food, good wine and pretty girls, O Lord we thank thee
Cardinal Basil Hume at annual dinner of Hawks Club, Cambridge

A woman's greatest weapon is man's imagination
Sophia Loren

When I was young and irresponsible I was young and irresponsible
George W. Bush Jr

Senescence begins
And middle age ends
The day your descendants
Outnumber your friends
Ogden Nash

Sign on the door of the meteorologist's office at a West Country naval air base: "Wet paint. Becoming drier later"

The Unenjoyed
Max Beerbohm's description of suffragettes

Most women are not as young as they are painted
Max Beerbohm: "A Defence of Cosmetics"

You can never be too rich or too thin
Wallis Simpson

There is only one race greater than the Jews, and that is the Derby
Victor Sassoon

Powell looks at me in Cabinet like Savanarola eyeing one of the more disreputable Popes
Harold Macmillan on Enoch Powell

"I. Pulham. Dentist"
Notice outside premises in Roundhay Road, Leeds

Knowing my luck, when my ship comes in I'll be at the airport
Anon

A friend in need is a friend to be avoided
Lord Salmon

A closed mouth gathers no feet
Anon

To keep your marriage brimming,
With love in the loving cup,
Whenever you're wrong, admit it;
Whenever you're right, shut up
Ogden Nash

Birth is the beginning of the end and death is nature's way of telling you to slow down
Terry Wogan, broadcaster

In love the only way to achieve victory is to run away
Napoleon

A psychopath knows the words but not the music
Anon

I love children but I can't bear them
Shakespeare

It takes a village to rear a child
Ashanti proverb

If you're in business, that's what you're doing
Margaret Blackwell

The trouble with the inscrutable Orient is that you can't scrute it
Roy Hudd

Treachery is not a matter of morals but of timing
Talleyrand

I have never yet known a man admit that he was either rich or asleep
Patrick O'Brian: "Master and Commander"

I am debarred from putting her in her place; she hasn't got one
Edith Sitwell

There is nothing like alcohol for removing the surface veneer
Furniture Repairers' Guide

There are no pockets in a shroud
You can't squeeze butter out of a fly
Arab proverbs

Diplomacy is the ability to tell a man to go to hell and make him look forward to the journey

One martini is too little, two is about right, three are not nearly enough
Dorothy Parker

A woman needs a man like a fish needs a bicycle
Gloria Steinham

Never catch a falling knife, never chase a runaway wife
Geordie saying

An orgy looks particularly alluring seen through the mists of righteous indignation
Malcolm Muggeridge

A man is ... better pleased when he has a good dinner on the table than when his wife talks Greek
Samuel Johnson

Face the front, speak clearly, and think dirty
Edith Evans's advice to aspiring actors

In war, the moral is to the physical as three is to one
Napoleon

The wooden walls are the best walls of this kingdom
Baron Coventry (1578-1640)

Do not do unto others as you would they should do unto you. Their tastes may not be the same
Bernard Shaw

His Grace returned from the war today and pleasured me twice in his top boots
Duchess of Marlborough (1660-1744)

Moderation is a fatal thing; nothing succeeds like excess
Oscar Wilde

The advantage of praising yourself is that you can lay it on thick and in the right places
Samuel Butler

A poet is an unhappy being whose heart is torn by secret sufferings but whose lips are so strangely formed that when the sighs and the cries escape them, they sound like beautiful music
A.L. Rowse

If two wrongs don't make a right, try three
Richard Nixon

Up lad; thews that lie and cumber
Sunlit pallets never thrive;
Morns abed and daylight slumber
Were not meant for man alive

Clay lies still, but blood's a rover;
Breath's a ware that will not keep.
Up, lad; when the journey's over
There'll be time enough to sleep
A.E. Housman: "Shropshire Lad"

Experto credite (Trust one who has been through it)
Virgil: Aeneid xi

Ille terrarum mihi praeter omnis angulus ridet
(That corner of the world smiles for me more than anywhere else)
Horace: Odes II vi

When the legend becomes fact, print the legend
John Ford

Haraka karaka haina baraka
(Hurry hurry has no profit *or* never rush your fences or you'll come
a cropper)
Swahili proverb

Storms make oaks take deeper root
George Herbert

Possessions lost - something lost. Honours lost - much lost.
Courage lost - everything lost
Goethe

If all the good people were clever
And all clever people were good
The world would be nicer than ever
We thought it possibly could

But somehow 'tis seldom or never
The two hit it off as they should
The good are so harsh to the clever
The clever so rude to the good
Elizabeth Wordsworth (1840-1882)

Let not the sun go down on your wrath
Ephesians IV.26

Il n'y a rien qui dure comme la provisoire
(Nothing lasts like the provisional)
French proverb

If you think you are doing a good job you may be comparing yourself with the wrong people

All philosophers are tyrannised by logic and logic by its nature is optimism
Nietzsche

A man's actions are the picture-book of his beliefs
Emerson

Perhaps I've been too interested in politics to be a good politician
Enoch Powell

"How would you like your hair cut?" his hairdresser asked Enoch Powell. "In complete silence" was the reply.

No man should be Viceroy of India to whom the office is an honour
Lord Curzon

I would never have made a politician because I don't believe I'm always right
Anon

The more you know, the fewer your competitors are

Yan tan tethera pethera pimp
(One two three four five)
Yorkshire shepherd's traditional count

You do not fatten a pig by weighing it
Russian saying

No one preaches better than the ant, and she says nothing
Benjamin Franklin

All the glory I claim in this world is that I have lived quietly
Montaigne

Nothing in life is to be feared. It is only to be understood
Marie Curie

Gratitude is the mother of all virtues
Cicero

My grandfather always said that living is like licking honey off a thorn
Louis Adamic

Success is an excellent training ground for failure. If at first you don't succeed your successor will
Anon

If at first you don't succeed, failure may be your style
Quentin Crisp

The race is not always to the swift, the battle is not always to the strong, but that's the way to bet
Damon Runyon

Buying cheap goods to save money is like stopping the clock to save time
Christmas cracker

Everything is in other hands, Lucillius. Time alone is ours
Seneca the Stoic

Nature, time and patience are the three great physicians
Bulgarian proverb

What is patriotism but the memory of the good things we ate in
our childhood?
Lin Yutang

How do I know my youth is spent?
Well, my get-up-and-go is got up and went!

The greatest calamity is not to have failed, but to have failed to try

Blessed are they who have nothing to say
And cannot be persuaded to say it

Never put off till tomorrow what you can do the day after
tomorrow just as well
Mark Twain

There is something ghostly in great art
Lafcadio Hearn

It is as hard to see oneself as to look backwards without turning
round
Thoreau

Il faut être profond en termes clairs et non pas en termes obscurs
(Profundity requires clarity of expression not obscurity)
Joubert

To a cricketer an optimist is a man who opens the batting
wearing sun-cream

One of Mandell Creighton's children, when asked what was going
to be done about the bishopric of Peterborough which had been
offered (1891) to his father, replied "Father is still praying, but
mother is packing our boxes"
Reginald Hine: "Confessions of an Uncommon Attorney"

La beauté de l'ange, la force du tigre et les ailes de l'aigle
(The beauty of an angel, the strength of a tiger and the wings of an
eagle)
Gabriele d'Annunzio's favourite phrase

Always remember that you are absolutely unique - just like everyone else
Meade's Maxim

Architecture in general is frozen music
Friedrich von Schelling 1809

So I'm asking you to send us a sample of the folding stuff - a bit of lettuce. Some long green ones. A pony would be nice; a big one even nicer; a monkey - very good indeed; a K truly happiness producing; and a couple of long-tailed bars best of all
John Cleese

A man is never so harmless as when in pursuit of money; and never so evil as when in pursuit of power
La Rochefoucauld

Life has two rules. Number one is never quit. Number two is always remember number one
Duke Ellington

Genius does what it must; talent does what it can
Owen Meredith: Last words of a Sensitive Second-rate Poet

The devil is in the detail
US saying

The happiness of your life depends upon the quality of your thoughts
Marcus Aurelius

Tact is the art of making a point without making an enemy

Do the best you can, and if you can, do better than other people
Thetis to her son Achilles

When life gives you lemons, make lemonade

On ne badine pas avec l'amour
(One does not trifle with love)
de Musset

Aliquando bonus dormitat
(The greatest men are sometimes caught napping)
Horace

Nothing is really work unless you would rather be doing something else
J.M. Barrie

Non est arbor solida nec fortis nisi in quam frequens ventas incurset (No tree is well-rooted and strong that has not been beaten by many winds)
Seneca de Providentia

The louder he talked of his honour, the faster we counted our spoons
R.W. Emerson

The wise man seeks perfection; only the fool expects to find it

Oh, give us your plain-dealing fellows,
Who never from honesty shrink,
Not thinking of all they shall tell us,
But telling us all that they think
Master's Song, Worshipful Company of Broderers

Great Spirit, teach me not to judge another until I have walked two
weeks in his moccasins
Red Indian prayer on bedroom mirror of Mr Speaker Wetherall

Quien a buen arbol se arrima buena sombra le corbija
(A fine tree gives good shade to him who leans against it)
Cervantes: "Don Quixote"

Gift is small
Grace is all

The mill cannot grind with water that has past
L. Doudney

The past is a foreign country; they do things differently there
L.P. Hartley

It's ying and yang; you give up one thing and take up another
Griff Rhys-Jones

The future isn't what it used to be
Yogi Bena, New York baseball star

It's always desirable to tell the truth, but seldom if ever necessary

Do not go gentle into that good night,
Old age should burn and rave at close of day.
Rage, rage against the dying of the light
Dylan Thomas

By swallowing evil words unsaid no one has yet harmed his
stomach
Winston Churchill

A clergyman being in want
Of a second-hand portable font,
Will exchange for the same
The portrait in frame
Of the Bishop-elect of Vermont
*Reputed to be an advertisement placed in the agony column of The Times
by Ronald Knox*

May the road rise to meet you,
May the wind be always at your back,
May the sun shine warm upon your face,
May the rain fall soft upon your fields.
And until we meet again,
May God hold you in the palm of his hand
An Irish Blessing

Everything in life is seven to five against
Damon Runyon

Simplicity, symmetry, continuity
The engineer's motto

It's not enough to succeed; other people must fail
Gore Vidal

Je vais chercher le grand peut-être
(I'm off to look for the big maybe)
Rabelais

His speeches in the House are always two coupons short of a pop-
up toaster
Matthew Parris, Parliamentary correspondent

Beauty is the handwriting of God
Charles Kingsley

Everyone is ignorant, but on different subjects
Will Rogers

Remember there's a difference between having to say something
and having something to say

Every contract is an act of distrust
Ortega y Gasset

If you can't convince them, confuse them
Harry S. Truman

Always be sincere, even if you don't mean it
Harry S. Truman

A man has to believe in something and I believe I'll have another drink
W.C. Fields

Life must be lived looking forward but can only be understood looking backward
Kierkegaard

Yes, I remember Adlestrop -
The name, because one afternoon
Of heat the express train drew up there
Unwontedly. It was late June.

The steam hissed. Someone cleared his throat.
No-one left and no-one came
On the bare platform. What I saw
Was Adlestrop - only the name.
Edward Thomas (1876-1917): "Adlestrop"

He has the right to criticize who has the heart to help
Abraham Lincoln

Management is the highest rate of change an organisation can stand
Sir John Harvey-Jones

Fraud is the way you get money into a company; stealing is the way you get it out
Sir Kenneth Cork

The City lives on rumour. Without rumour there wouldn't be a Stock Exchange
Sir Kenneth Cork

I know that that's a secret, for it's whispered everywhere
Congreve: "Love for Love"

The Press lives by disclosures
Editor, The Times, 1852

You can get much further with a kind word and a gun than you can with just a kind word
Al Capone, quoted in The Independent

Opinion polls are like swimsuits; what they reveal can be less interesting than what they conceal
The Times, November 6, 1999

Winning is the science of being totally prepared

Experience is what you get when you can't get what you want
L. Boots: "Loose Talk, 1980"

Experience is what enables you to recognise a mistake every time you repeat it

It is a step towards chaos when argument begins
Chinese proverb

Eheu fugaces labuntur anni
(Alas the fleeting years are slipping by)
Horace: Odes

You never get a second chance to make a first impression
Advertisement for shampoo

These are my principles, and if you don't like them, I have others
Old adage

Wise persons never let yesterday's mistakes use up too much of today

Adopt the pace of nature; her secret is patience
Emerson

The definition of an honest man is one whose price is too high
Tiny Rowland

In the 1970s *The Times* ran a poster campaign to increase sales. This generated a number of memorable captions:
    Truth will in
    Read our minds
    Wordsworth
    We never make capital out of minor issues
    An eye for a lie
    A tooth for the truth
    Tax yourself
    Pioneers in sound recording
    We repay you with interest
    Get a second opinion first

Evangelism is one beggar telling another beggar where to find bread
B.T. Niles

A spade will be as great a necessity as a rifle
Sir John French

Once in finesse of fiddles found I ecstasy,
In a flash of gold heels on the hard pavement
Now see!
That warmth's the very stuff of poesy
O God make small
The old star-eaten blanket of the sky
That I may fold it round me
And in comfort lie
T.E. Holmes: "Fantasia of a Fallen Gentleman on a Cold Bitter Night"
(Poems on the Underground)

The worst is not always the most certain
Paul Claudel

If a man thinks well of you, make his thoughts come true
Arabian proverb

He who smiles rather than rages is always the stronger
Japanese proverb

Be careful of what you pray for; you might get it
Spanish proverb

Institutions are in trouble when their critics are unloving and their
lovers are uncritical
George Kennan

He draweth out the thread of his verbosity finer than the staple of
his argument
Shakespeare: "Love's Labours Lost"

I am never less alone than when alone
William Cowper

Then many a lad I liked is dead
And many a lass grown old
And as the lesson strikes my head
My weary heart grows old

But wine awhile drives off despair
Nay, bids a hope remain,
And that I think's a reason fair
To fill my glass again
Captain Charles Morris (1739-1832): " Toper's Apology"

Being a philosopher, I have a problem for every solution
Robert Zend (1929-1985), Canadian Post

Giant's Causeway is worth seeing but not worth going to see
Samuel Johnson

Love thy neighbour, but build a fence. Love God, but don't neglect the Devil
Russian proverb cited by Peter Ustinov

I have never been hurt by anything I didn't say
Calvin Coolidge

Her breasts were her erroneous zones
John Diamond

Be kind. Remember everyone you meet is fighting a hard battle
T.H. Thompson

Bad habits are like a comfortable bed; easy to get into, but hard to get out of

Nam risu inepto res ineptior nulla est
(There's nothing sillier than a silly smile)
Catullus: Carmina xxxix

Keep your fears to yourself but share your courage with others
Stevenson

At Christmas a capon
At Michaelmas a goose
And somewhat else at New Year's tide
For fear the lease flies loose
Traditional rhyme cited by Brian Redhead

Politics is a choice between the disastrous and the unpalatable

Every public action which is not customary, either is wrong, or, if
it is right, is a dangerous precedent. It follows that nothing should
ever be done for the first time
Francis Cornford 1908: "Microcosmographia Academica"

A committee meeting is a group of the unwilling, picked from the
unfit, to do the unnecessary
Various attributions: origin unknown

Facts are the shadows that statements cast on things
Strawson

He who doesn't play cards has an unhappy old age
Talleyrand

I live on good soup, not fine language
Molière

Those who live in glass houses should not get undressed with the light on
Street saying

The dog that trots about finds a bone
Gypsy proverb cited by George Borrow: "Bible in Spain"

And dark scents whisper, and dim waves creep to me
Gleam like a woman's hair, stretch out and rise
And new stars burn into the ancient skies
Over the murmurous soft Hawaiian sea
Rupert Brooke: "Hawaii"

Better a witty fool than a foolish wit
Shakespeare: "Twelfth Night"

He who educates a man educates a man; he who educates a woman educates a nation
Malcolm X

I am an old man and have known a great many troubles, but most of them have never happened
Mark Twain

"I'm not denying that women are fools. God almighty made 'em to match the men"
George Eliot: Mrs Poyser: "Mill on the Floss"

Charm is an art developed by men to spare them the risks of the fight
Leanda de Lisle in the Daily Mail

All things considered, I'd rather be in Philadelphia
Epitaph on gravestone of WC Fields

There's nothing I wouldn't do for him. There's nothing he wouldn't do for me. We have known each other for 40 years. We've done nothing for each other
Kerr

My dear Reggie,
In these dark days man tends to look for little shafts of light that spill from heaven. My days are probably darker than yours and I need, my God I do, all the light I can get. But I am a decent fellow and I do not want to be mean and selfish about what little brightness is shed upon me from time to time. So I propose to share with you a tiny flash that has illuminated my sombre life and tell you that God has given me a new Turkish colleague whose card tells me that he is called Mustapha Kunt.

We all feel like that, Reggie, now and then, especially when Spring is upon us, but few of us would care to put it on our cards. It takes a Turk to do that.
Sir Archibald Clerk Kerr
HM Ambassador, HM Embassy, Moscow
Letter written to the 15th Earl of Pembroke at the Foreign Office on April 6, 1943, two months after the German surrender at Stalingrad and cited in The Sunday Telegraph, August 29, 1993, the 50-year rule then having expired

Leave it alone
Lord Rosebery

"What are the effects of the French Revolution?"
"It is too early yet to say."
Zhou Enlai

Adultery is the application of democracy to love
H.L. Mencken

The road of excess leads to the palace of wisdom
William Blake

You deprive me of solitude without affording me company
Madame de Sévigné

If you come to a fork in the road - take it
Street saying

Baseball is 90 per cent physical; the other half is mental
Yogi Bena, New York baseball star

She's just divine, but I wonder if her elevator goes all the way to
the top floor
US lady about Princess Diana

Whatever it was that this actress never had, she still hasn't got it
New York Times 1945 on Loretta Young

You should try everything once - except incest and Morris dancing
Sir Thomas Beecham

The retail business is detail business
Simon Marks

Life's a beach
Martine Aubry

It doesn't matter what you do in the bedroom as long as you don't
do it in the street and frighten the horses
Mrs Patrick Campbell (1865-1940)

Take a drop kick for Jesus through the goal-posts of life
Hank Wangford, Country and Western singer and gynaecologist

The longer the spoke the bigger the tyre
Anon

Climb high, climb far
Your goal the sky,
Your aim a star
Inscription on memorial at Williamstown Ma USA

What is important is not the man in my life but the life in my man
Mae West

I don't care what people write about me as long as it's not true
Katharine Hepburn

What old age lacks is not the desire but the ability
Harold Nicolson

Chastity is not chastity in an old man, but a disability to be unchaste
John Donne

After the age of 50 no man should speak in public for longer than he can make love
Hegel

If I had known I was going to live so long, I would have taken better care of myself
Bob Hope

You ask "may we smoke?" We say "Yes. You may smoke. For all we care, you may burn"
Robert Ricketts, Footlights, Cambridge

A pair of twins is guarding a fork road. One twin always tells the truth; the other always tells lies. What question would you ask to ascertain which road was safe? The question is: "If I ask your brother which is the safe road, what would he say?". Whatever the answer, take the other road
Attribution unknown

Small dwellings discipline the mind; large ones weaken it
Leonardo da Vinci

The test of a gentleman is that he is never unwittingly rude to anyone
Charles Dickens

A wise man knows everything
A shrewd man knows everybody

In life it's not who you know, it's whom you know

And that inverted bowl we call the sky
Where under crawling coop'd we live and die
Lift not thy hands to It for help - for It
Rolls impotently on as Thou or I
Omar Khayyam

Better is a dinner of herbs where love is, than a stalled ox and hatred therewith
Proverbs 15:17

Total abstinence is far easier than perfect moderation
St Augustine

The great age of European expansion was no out-pouring of pent-up dynamism. It was launched from the insecure edges of a contracting civilisation. It was a slow and sometimes tortured recovery from the crisis of the Middle Ages
Felipe Fernandez-Armesto: "Millennium" p.155

One of the drawbacks of freedom is that free choices are regularly made for the worst, ever since the setting of an important precedent in Eden
Ibid., p.493

If you want to interest a Frenchman in a game, tell him it's war. If you want to interest an Englishman in war, tell him it's a game
Duke of Wellington

Manners are especially the need of the plain; the pretty can get away with anything
Evelyn Waugh

What I see tires me, and what I don't see worries me
Madam de Sévigné

I am more or less happy when being praised, not very uncomfortable when being abused, but I have moments of uneasiness when being explained
Balfour

I am a traditionalist with an appetite for change
Giscard d'Estaing

Tradition is the democracy of the dead
G.K. Chesterton: "Ethics of Elfland"

One draws from the well of language many a thought one does not have
Lichtenberg

The day you have nothing to worry about the pop stars have nothing to sing

If you want some flotsam I've got some; if you want some jetsam I'll get some
Ogden Nash

Qui cantat bis orat
(He who sings says a double prayer)
John Youlden

Indecision is the key to flexibility

One must be poor to appreciate the luxury of giving
George Eliot

A working writer's attitude to critics is that of a flowerbed to cats

Life is what happens to you when you're busy making other plans
John Lennon

My father was the better swasher, but I was the better buckler
Douglas Fairbanks Jr

God is a circle the centre of which is everywhere, but which has no circumference
Empedocles

Some people are troubled by things in the Bible which they cannot understand, but as for me, I am troubled by the things I can understand
Mark Twain

If things are not as you like, like them as they are
Jewish saying

The man who marries for money earns it
Jewish saying

Fishing is not a matter of life and death; it's much more important than that

Be joyful, seek the best, and let the sparrows chirp
Pope John XXIII

At a dinner party, one should eat wisely but not too well, and talk well but not too wisely
Somerset Maugham

The art of being wise is the art of knowing what to overlook

Happiness is horizontal
Ronnie Corbett

He that will not apply new remedies must expect new evils, for time is the greatest innovator
Francis Bacon

Buy wine with an apple; sell it with cheese
French saying

Stay me with flagons, comfort me with apples
Song of Solomon

Be kind to people, but keep your end up
John Galsworthy: Forsyte Saga

Contraceptives should be used on all conceivable occasions
Spike Milligan

C'est un grand habilité que de savoir cacher son habilité
(The cleverest thing is to know how to conceal your cleverness)
La Rochefoucauld

Never chase the lass you fancy; always chase the lass who fancies
you
Yorkshire saying

"Rodney, has Del Boy ever suffered with pleurisy?"
"No. Only when he's tried to spell it!"
BBC: "Only Fools and Horses"

The rows and rows
Of "Mon Repos"
John Betjeman: "Suburbia"

The secret of enjoying money is to make it first and make it last
Evening Standard

Life is a sexually transmitted disease
Faber: "Book of Fevers"

He who would search for pearls must dive below
John Dryden

I was brought up to believe that it was very insulting to sleep with
your wife or any lady. A gentleman stays eagerly awake. He sleeps
at his work
Alan Ayckbourn

Nothing should ever be done for the first time
Bernard Shaw

We must stand for something lest we fall for anything

What the Gods call gallantry
And men adultery
Is much more common
When the weather's sultry
Byron

It is always Judas who writes the biography
Oscar Wilde

Time is nature's way of stopping everything happening at once
Anon

Flattery is like tobacco; it doesn't do you any harm provided you
don't inhale
Tom Williams

I believe in moderation in everything - especially moderation

Moderation is a fatal thing. Nothing succeeds like excess
Oscar Wilde

De mortuis nil nisi bunkum
H.L. Mencken

So little done, so much to do
Cecil Rhodes, on his death bed

Un anglais, c'est un gentilhomme
Deux Anglais, c'est un club
Trois Anglais, c'est un empire
French saying

Friends come and go, enemies accumulate
Anon

Experience is stupidity hardened by practice
London taxi driver

If you think education is expensive, try ignorance
Derek Bok

Work, for the night is coming on
Anna Louise Walker: "Leaves from the Backwoods" 1861

When the angels play for God, they play Bach; when they play for
themselves, they play Mozart
Karl Barth

The ancient Goths of Germany had a wise custom of debating
matters of state twice - once drunk, once sober. Drunk that their
councils might not want vigour; and sober that they might not
want discretion
Laurence Sterne: "Tristram Shandy" volume 2, chapter XVI

It seems to have been a custom among the Zulus to put the king to
death the moment he got wrinkles or grey hair
Sir James Frazer (1854-1941): "The Golden Bough"

For the triumph of evil it is only necessary that good men do
nothing
Edmund Burke

A civilised tax system breathes through its loopholes
G.S.A. Wheatcroft

A rut is like a grave only longer
Lord Leverhulme

Parliamentary democracy is the worst system that anyone can imagine, except for all the other kinds of government that have ever been tried
Winston Churchill

Government is the only institution that can take a valuable commodity like paper and make it worthless by applying ink
Ludwig van Moses

Doing what's right isn't the problem; it's knowing what's right
Lyndon Johnson

If thine aunt had cojones she would be thine uncle
Ernest Hemingway

There's no art
Can find the mind's construction in the face
Shakespeare: "Macbeth"

Direct action is the Magna Carta of barbarism
Street saying

He who dies rich dies disgraced
Andrew Carnegie

All passes; art alone
Enduring stays to us.
The bust outlasts the thorne,
The coin Tiberius
H.A. Dobson

There is no excellent beauty that hath not some strangeness in the proportion
Francis Bacon

No rich man is ugly
Zsa Zsa Gabor

L'amour c'est qui se passe entre deux personnes qui s'aiment
(Love is what happens between two people who are in love)
Roger Vailland

America is the first society to move straight from barbarism to
decadence without touching civilisation on the way
Bernard Shaw

The most significant fact of modern history is that America speaks
English
Ludwig von Bismarck

America and England are two nations divided by a common language
Attributed to Winston Churchill

The degree of one's emotions varies inversely with one's knowledge of the facts. The less you know, the hotter you get
Bertrand Russell

Life copies art
Oscar Wilde

No man is demolished but by himself
Thomas Bentley (1693-1742)

Il n'y a point de heros pour son valet de chambre
(No man is a hero to his valet)
Madame Cornuel 1728

There are only three occupations that befit a gentleman - war, cards and women
Somerset Maugham: "Ashenden"

He trivialises everything he touches
The Times on Harold Wilson

A man's opinion is worth no more than his information
Paul Getty senior

It is better to do a good deed near home than to travel a thousand miles to burn incense
Chinese proverb

I feel better now that I've given up hope

One of the most important trips a man can make is that involved in meeting the other fellow half way

Never trust a man who
  *   hunts South of the Thames
  *   has a waxed moustache
  *   eats soup for lunch
Sir James Richards (1907-1992), architectural historian and critic, quoting his father

He done his dam' best.
Angels couldn't do no more
Epitaph on Klondike miner seen by Bret Harte

Everything flows and nothing stays
Heraclitus: "Plato"

They told me, Heraclitus, they told me you were dead,
They brought me bitter news to hear and bitter tears to shed
William Cory: "Heraclitus"

When you're right no one remembers; when you're wrong no one forgets
William Addison

People who matter don't mind, people who mind don't matter
Attributed to diplomat's wife discussing order of precedence in seating arrangements at an ambassadorial dinner

Even victors are by victories undone
Dryden: Epistles

Grow old along with me; the best is yet to be
Robert Browning: "Rabbi ben Ezra"

L'esprit de l'escalier
Denis Diderot (1713-1784); a phrase which encapsulates the notion that one always thinks after the event of the right bon mot

Dis aliter visum
(It seemed otherwise to the gods)
Virgil: Aeneid. vi. 428

Life is the only thing that's given to you free
Lucretius

There's no fool like an old fool;
You can't beat experience
Jacob M Braude: "Treasure of Wit and Humour"

Nostalgie de la boue (Homesickness for the gutter)
Emile Angier (1820-1889)

Enfers c'est les autres (Hell is other people)
Jean Paul Sartre

She had every virtue and only one vice; she was intolerable
Jane Austen

You catch more flies with honey than with vinegar
West Country saying

L'embarras des richesses
(The wider the choice the more difficult it is)
Abbe d'Allaindal 1726

If you knock a book against your head and there is a hollow sound, it doesn't necessarily mean there's nothing in the book
Margaret Bacon

You have tasted a whole worm,
You have hissed my mystery lectures,
You were fighting a liar in the quadrangle.
You will leave by the town drain
Attributed to W.A. Spooner, Warden of New College Oxford 1902-24

... a collection of sound and original ideas. The only trouble with them is that none of the sound ideas are original and none of the original ideas are sound
Harold Macmillan on policies of the Liberal party 1960

The world is composed of takers and givers. The takers may eat better, but the givers sleep better

Bis dat qui cito dat
(He gives twice who gives quickly)
Attributed to Publilius Syrus

I cannot hear what you say for the noise of who you are is ringing in my ears
Chinese proverb

Et venio in campos et lata praetoria memoriae
(And I come to the fields and wide palaces of memory)
St Augustine

The deep slumber of the decided opinion
T.H. Green

It is inadvisable to leap a chasm in two stages
David Lloyd George

He who travels much doubts many things
African proverb

Take the bitter with the better
James Cagney

My right to disagree with you stops where your nose begins
Judge Learned Hand

Beauty in architecture comprises symmetry, harmony and proportion
Vitrurius

A man cannot participate in that which he cannot understand; he can only interfere
Script of film "Participation" 1977

A rose is a rose is a rose is a rose
Gertrude Stein

A weed is a plant whose virtues have not yet been discovered
Emerson

Mopani says that the four most beautiful things in the world are
thunder, lightning, a falling star and the roar of a lion
Laurens van der Post: "A Far-off Place"

When you reorganise you bleed
G.F. Fiennes

There are only two lasting bequests we can give our children - one
is roots, the other wings

City government is of the people by the rascals for the rich
Lincoln Steffence

Man's capacity for evil makes democracy necessary and man's
capacity for good makes democracy possible
Reinhold Niebuhr

All popular violence arises from popular suffering
Sully, Minister to Henry IV of France

To get power, sell your mother; once you have power there are
many ways of getting her back
Ashanti proverb

I want everything to be spoken; silence is for saints or slaves, like
suffering
Melvyn Bragg: "The Silken Net", p.140

Patience et longeur de temps font plus que force ni rage
(Patience and the passing of the years have more effect than violence and anger)
La Fontaine

I know I am not very bright, but I do know that I am always right
J.M. Barrie: "Quality Street"

By winds the sea is lashed to storm, but if it be unvexed it is of all things most amenable
Solon

Soon the stars were great and loud with light until the sky trembled like an electric bell
Laurens van der Post: "Heart of a Hunter", p.37

Excellence invites the malice of the mediocre

The more things a man is ashamed of, the more respectable he is
Bernard Shaw: "Man and Superman", Act 1

May you live in memorable times
Chinese curse

Experience enables one to make the same mistake again without getting caught
Oscar Wilde

Matrimony has many pains, but celibacy has no pleasures
Samuel Johnson

The man who has never done a foolish thing is not as wise as he thinks
La Rochefoucauld

The difference between a politician and a statesman is that a politician is the leader of your party, a statesman is the leader of mine
Lord Eldon

Every Prime Ministers needs a Willie
Margaret Thatcher on Lord Whitelaw

We must not prejudge the past
Lord Whitelaw

It is better to remain silent and be thought a fool than to speak and remove all doubt
Alan King-Hamilton

The pleasure is momentary, the position ridiculous, and the expense damnable
Earl of Chesterfield on sex

Il n'y a que le premier pas qui coute
(It's only the first step that counts)
Marquise du Deffand 1763

Truth is a moving target
T.E. Lawrence

To my deaf aid I'm accustomed
To my dentures I'm resigned
I can cope with my bifocals
But how I miss my mind!
Attributed to Lord Home of the Hirsel

Prends moi tel que je suis (Take me as I am)
Ricketts family motto

Fronti nulla fides (Trust not to outward show)
Cripps family motto

Life is a tragedy when seen in close-up, but a comedy in long-shot
Charles Chaplin

Life is a comedy to those who think, a tragedy to those who feel
Horace Walpole 1769

The effectiveness of assertion is the alpha and omega of style
Bernard Shaw

Things will be aye some way
Scottish saying

What really flatters a man is that you think him worth flattering

Les grands seigneurs ont des plaisirs; le peuple a de la joie
(The lords have pleasures; the people have joy)

You can tell a wise man by the number of women around him
Zulu proverb

When you get to the end of your rope, tie a knot and hang on
Yorkshire saying

Roses are red
Violets are bluish
If it wasn't for Christmas
We'd all be Jewish
Joyce Grenfell's Christmas card 1977

Capitalism is the exploitation of man by man. Communism is the
exact opposite

If the wind brings you a gift, put a stone on it
Ashanti proverb

Los huespedes y la pesca. A los tres dias apestan!
(After three days your guests resemble fish - they smell)
Spanish proverb

A man is not old when his hair goes grey,
A man is not old when his teeth decay,
But a man is ready for his long, last sleep
When his mind makes appointments that his body cannot keep
Street rhyme

The procession marches in the mind
Catalan proverb

It is interesting to note how the meaning of words has changed over the years. When James II first saw St Paul's Cathedral he called it amusing, awful and artificial. He meant that it was pleasing to look at, deserving of awe and full of skilful artifice.
Simeon Potter: "Our language"

No gastes todo lo que tienes
Porque el que gasta lo que tiene
Muchas veces gasta lo que no tiene
(Don't spend all you've got, for the man who spends all he's got, often spends what he hasn't got)
Spanish saying

Frank Lloyd Wright, when asked which was his best work, answered "the next one" and when asked which of Brahms' symphonies he most liked, replied "the one I heard last"

If only you could see inside me you would be blinded by the vision I have of you
Laurens van der Post: "The Seed and the Sower", p.238

One is as wretched, so to speak, in Cap d'Antibes as round the Wrekin
Patrick Purpoole

Art is like reality - it consists in drawing the line somewhere

O yes, I saw sweet beauty in her face ...
I saw her coral lips to move
And with her breath she did perfume the air;
Sacred and sweet was all I saw in her
Shakespeare: "Taming of the Shrew", Act 1, Scene 1

Difficile est longum subito deponere amorem
(`Tis difficult at once to drop old-standing love)
Catullus: Carmina, Book 76

To hear is to learn
To see is to remember
To do is to understand

A friend is one
to whom one may pour
Out all the contents
Of one's heart
Chaff and grain together
Knowing that the
Gentlest of hands
Will take and sift it,
Keep what is worth keeping
And with a breath of kindness
Blow the rest away
Arabian saying

The fickleness of the women I love is matched only by the
constancy of the women who love me
Bernard Shaw

Never love a man too much; that is to give him too much power
Ibid

"What do you consider the greatest obstacle to the emancipation
of women?" Louis Wilkinson once asked Bernard Shaw. "Lust," he
replied

Many receive advice; only the wise profit by it
Publilius Syrus

I always talk bawdy at dinner, then everyone can join in
Horace Walpole

He who knows best knows how little he knows
Thomas Jefferson

Dulce est desipere in loco
(It is lovely in the proper place to forget one's wisdom)
Horace: Odes IV. xii. 27

Not to be a republican at 20 is proof of want of a heart; to be one at 30 is proof of want of a head
Guizot

Riots are the voice of the unheard
Martin Luther King

In October
When winter the lodger the sod
Came a-knocking at our door
I set in a store
Of biscuit and whisky
You filled the hot water bottle with tears
And we went to bed until spring
Anon

Hell is full of musical amateurs; music is the brandy of the damned
Bernard Shaw: "Major Barbara"

The love of truth is the faintest of human passions
A.E. Housman

The desire not to look an old fool has become stronger than lust
Malcolm Muggeridge

It is not difficult to govern Italy; it is merely futile
Benito Mussolini

It is necessary to take your job very seriously, yourself not at all
Spencer Tracy

The pessimist sees the difficulty in every opportunity; the optimist the opportunity in every difficulty
L.P. Jacks

Governments are more the effect than the cause of what we are
S.T. Coleridge

Money enables us to get what we want instead of what other people think we want
Bernard Shaw

Democracy gives every man the right to be his own oppressor
J.R. Lowell

The fact that majorities have been wrong must not blind us to the fact that majorities have not usually been entirely wrong
Herbert Spencer

The constitutional king is king in order that no one else may be king
Sir George Cornewall Lewis (1806-1863)

I never read a book before reviewing it; it prejudices one so
Sydney Smith (1771-1845)

Si non e vero, e molto ben trovato
(If it isn't true, it's a happy invention)
Italian 16th century saying

You may depend upon it, all lives out of London are mistakes,
more or less grievous, but mistakes
Sydney Smith (1771-1845)

If it moves get on board
Indian street saying

No one needs a holiday more than a man who has just had one
Old saying

Fair Cloacina, goddess of this place,
Look on thy suppliant with a smiling face.
Soft, yet cohesive, let my offering flow,
Not rudely swift nor insolently slow
Attributed to Byron: "Poem for a small place"

He's 50 from the neck up; 14 from the waist down
Shirley MacLaine of her brother Warren Beatty

My doctor gave me six months to live, and then when I couldn't
pay the bill, he gave me six months more
Walter Mathau

I never mind my wife having the last word. In fact, I'm delighted
when she gets to it
Walter Mathau

Men create the problems of the world, analyse them and then leave
it to women to solve them

The thing is in this life, you can know a great deal about
something, and still be wrong
Sir Leonard Hutton

Ou sont les neiges d'antan? (Where are the snows of yesteryear?)
Francois Villon

Why art thou silent? Is thy love a plant
Of such weak fibre that the treacherous air
Of absence withers what was once so fair?
Is there no debt to pay, no boon to grant?
William Wordsworth: "To a Distant Friend"

A careless shoe-string, in whose tie
I see a wild civility,
Do more bewitch me, than when art
Is too precise in every part
Robert Herrick: "Delight in Disorder"

My name is Benjamin Jowett,
All there is to know I know it.
I am the Master of Balliol College,
What I know not is not knowledge.

I am the Dean[1] of Christ Church, Sir;
This is my wife; look well at her.
She is the Broad and I am the High,
And we are the University

I am rather tall and stately,
And I care not very greatly
What you say and what you do.
I'm Mackail[2], and who are you?

---

1. *Liddell*
2. *Professor, Balliol College*

I AM NOT THERE
Do not stand at my grave and weep,
I am not there; I do not sleep.
I am a thousand winds that blow,
I am the diamond glints on snow.
I am the sunlight on ripened grain,
I am the gentle autumn rain.
When you awaken in the morning's hush
I am the swift uplifting rush
Of quiet birds in circled flight.
I am the soft stars that shine at night.
Do not stand at my grave and cry.
I am not there; I did not die
Anon

Threescore and fifteen. Honour the wit who sings
Harmoniously; the scholar wise in lore
Of cloughs and choughs and butterflies and things
Macbeth omitted from his auguries.
Admirers all we celebrate and praise
Seventy-five ripe years, and wish you many more
Acrostic written by Anne Ridler, for Sir Arthur (Tom) Norrington's 75th birthday, October 27, 1974 (by kind permission of Humphrey Norrington)

FAREWELL
Because of you we will be glad and gay,
Remembering you, we will be brave and strong
And hail the advent of each dangerous day
And meet the last adventure with a song
Maurice Baring

A LOOK AT THE LAW

No man would be a judge on the condition of being obliged to be
totally a judge
Samuel Johnson

I know not whether Laws be right
Or whether Laws be wrong
All that we know who lie in gaol
Is that the wall is strong
Oscar Wilde: "Ballad of Reading Gaol"

Justice is the insurance we have on our lives and property;
obedience is the premium we pay for it
William Penn

Do right and fear no man; don't write and fear no woman
Motto of the former Divorce Division

Our stability is but balance, and wisdom lies
In masterful administration of the unforeseen
Robert Bridges (1844-1930): "The Testament of Beauty"

It is difficult to be accurate when one is trying to be fair
Derek Clarkson

Justice is a splendid thing, but you must not expect justice from this
life
An American judge

Where secrecy begins justice ends
Edmund Burke

Nothing meritorious is ever achieved by the effluxion of time
Lord Merrivale

Inner for the rich man
Middle for the poor
Lincoln's for the gentleman
Gray's Inn for the boor
Traditional Inns of Court rhyme

The legal profession is divided between those who understand what law is, and those who also understand what law is for
The Times

Men are not hanged for stealing horses; they are hanged so that horses may not be stolen
Lord Halifax (17th century)

Festinatio justitiae est noverea infortunii
(The hurry of justice is the step-mother of misfortune)
John Bouvier: "A Law Dictionary adapted to the Constitution and Laws of the USA" 1856

Fill the seats of justice with good men, but not so absolute in goodness as to forget what human frailty is
Sir Thomas Noon Talfourd

For the food by which we live, and for the law by which we live in peace, may the Lord make us truly thankful
Ven Thomas Barfett, Lay Sheriff of London's Chaplain July 1977

The age-old causes of crime are the desire for easy money, greed, passion, lust and cruelty
Lord Goddard, Lord Chief Justice

Fraud and deceit abound in these more than in former times
Sir Edward Coke, 1602

I not deny
The jury, passing on a prisoner's life
May in the sworn twelve have a thief or two
Guiltier than him they try
Shakespeare: "Measure for Measure"

The primary conditions for success at the Bar are to live like a hermit and work like a horse
Lord Eldon

Life at the Bar is no bed of roses. It is either all bed and no roses or all roses and no bed
Valentine Holmes

To succeed at the Bar one needs integrity, common sense and a good digestion
Lord Atkin

I begin to think that the tardy justice of the Chancellor is better than the swift injustice of his deputy
Samuel Romilly of Lord Eldon

Don't make the mistake of thinking that when a judge is silent he is thinking; he is just re-arranging his prejudices
Terry Wogan, broadcaster

Same with judges - you stick them in a uniform to make it clear it's the law of the land you're up against and not just a prejudiced old man; and if only they didn't sound off so while giving sentence, you might even go right on believing it
Katharine Whitehorn: The Observer Review

The acme of judicial distinction is to look a lawyer in the eyes for two hours and not hear a word he says
Chief Justice Marshall (USA)

The execution of the laws is more important than the making of them
Thomas Jefferson

The best way to get rid of a bad law is to enforce it
Judge King, Federal Judge, Hawaii

It is the boast of the law of England that it affords equal security and protection to the high and the low, to the rich and the poor
William Pitt the Younger; speech in House of Commons, February 1, 1793

The part of a judge in hearing are four: to direct the evidence; to moderate length, repetition or impertinency of speech; to recapitulate, select and collate the material points of that which hath been said; and to give rule or sentence. Whatever is above these is too much, and proceedeth of glory and willingness to speak, or of impatience to hear, or of shortness of memory, or of want of a stayed and equal attention
Mr Justice Grove at an Academy dinner, May 7, 1881

A well-known judge at the Old Bailey had two cards before him on his desk on which were written, "You are paid to be patient" and "Keep your mouth shut"

Against all law and evidence
The prisoner was acquitted
The judge exclaimed "Is common sense
To jurors not permitted?"
The prisoner's counsel rose and bowed:
"Your Honour why this fury?
By law the judge is not allowed
To sit upon the jury"
Ambrose Bierce: "Enlarged Devil's Dictionary"

The Chairman of Quarter Sessions dispenses the law of the land solely by virtue of owning it. All questions of fact he decides for himself. Questions of law he leaves to the jury
Mr Justice Darling: "Scintillae Juris"

Injustice is relatively easy to bear; what stings is justice
H.L. Mencken

Judex damnatur ubi nocens absolvitur
(The judge is condemned when the guilty party is acquitted)
Publilius Syrus; Sententia 247

A lawyer is someone willing to spend every penny you have to prove he's right
Graffiti at Swiss Cottage

In the USA a judge is a lawyer who once knew a politician

May your life be filled with lawyers
Maya (Mexico) curse

The good judge:
DOES NOT: dither over decisions
           have a short temper
IS NOT: impatient
           intellectually arrogant
IS: comfortable
           punctual
           affable
           firm
Mr Justice Tucker, address to Conference of the Bar, October 1994

The prime attribute of a judge is judgment
Lord Justice Roskill

A judge should by nature have the qualities of humility, humanity and humour

In Germany under the law, everything is prohibited, except that which is permitted. In France, under the law, everything is permitted except that which is prohibited. In Russia, under the law, everything is prohibited including that which is permitted. And in Italy, under the law, everything is permitted, especially that which is prohibited
Newton Minow, former Chairman Federal Communications Commission

O Lord, fill my mouth with worth while stuff,
And nudge me when I've said enough
A barrister's prayer

A civil law judge cannot speak, a common law judge cannot read

Two things remain in my mind about Lord Dunedin (Lord President of the Court of Session). He was never afraid to show he had changed his mind during an argument. And perhaps more significant to me was his manner of giving judgment. He would come up with some scrappy notes and weigh in. His grammar was lamentable; syntax meant nothing to him. But try as you would it was impossible to mistake his meaning. So I thought if ever it comes to my turn clarity must come first before - long before -

elegance or profundity. And for me that meant avoiding long woolly Latin words and sticking to good sturdy short Anglo-Saxon ones
Lord Reid at his retirement dinner, Middle Temple Hall

It is the duty of counsel to assist the judge by simplification and concentration and not to advance a multitude of ingenious arguments in the hope that out of 10 bad points the judge will be capable of fashioning a winner
Lord Templeman: Ashmore v. Corporation of Lloyds (1992) 1 WLR 446

Lawyers are to language what vandals are to telephone kiosks
Theodore Dalrymple

Le mauvais goût mène aux crimes
(Crime is a side-effect of bad taste)
Stendhal

A CONSPECTUS OF LEGALESE

A short lease means a lease which is not a long lease
Income Tax Act 1952 s.172(1)

The Marriage Act 1983 (Commencement) Order 1984
1. This Order may be cited as the Marriage Act (Commencement) Order 1984
2. The Marriage Act 1983 shall come into force on 1st May 1984
Explanatory Note
This Order brings the Marriage Act 1983 into force on 1st May 1984

Subject to subs.(4) of this section, subss.(3) and (4) of s.25 of this Act shall apply where the provisions of s.23 of this Act have effect as applied by subs.(1) of this section as they apply where those provisions have effect as applied by subs.(1) or subs.(2) of the said s.25.
Land Compensation Act 1961, s.26(3)

For the purpose of this Part of this Schedule a person over pensionable age, not being an insured person, shall be treated as an employed person if he would be an insured person were he under pensionable age and would be an employed person were he an insured person
National Insurance Act 1964, Schedule 1, Part II

If a right to acquire shares in a body corporate is assigned or released in whole or in part for a consideration which consists of or comprises another right to assign shares in that or any other body corporate, that right shall not be treated as consideration for the assignment or release, but this section shall apply in relation to it as it applies in relation to the right assigned or released and as if the consideration for its acquisition did not include the value of the right assigned or released but did include the amount or value of

the consideration given for the grant of the right assigned or released so far as that has not been offset by any valuable consideration for the assignment or release other than the consideration consisting of the other right
Finance Act 1966, s.5(3)

In these Regulations -
(a) except in the case of a dipped beam headlamp, a main beam headlamp, and a front fog lamp, a reference to one lamp includes any combination of two or more lamps, whether identical or not, having the same function and emitting light of the same colour, if it comprises devices, the projection of the aggregate light-emitting surface of which in a vertical plane perpendicular to the median longitudinal plane of the vehicle occupies 60% or more of the smallest rectangle circumscribing the projections of those light-emitting surfaces
Road Vehicle Lighting Regulations 1971, Regulation 1(a)

Deductions from total income under Chapter 2 of Part 1 of the Taxes Act shall, in the first instance, be disregarded in determining what income is chargeable as investment income and what income is not so chargeable; and shall then be chargeable as investment income not so chargeable before reducing any income so chargeable
Finance Act 1971, s.34(4)

Where ... a period consisting entirely of days of absence from the United Kingdom ("the relevant period") comes to an end and there have previously been one or more qualifying periods, the relevant period and the (or, if more than one, the last) qualifying period together with the intervening days between those periods shall be treated as a single qualifying period provided that: (a) there are no more than 62 intervening days; and (b) the number of days in the resulting periods which are not days of absence from the United

Kingdom does not exceed one sixth of the total number of days in
that period
Finance Act 1977, Schedule 7, para.3

An enactment in which s.31(6) and (7) of the Criminal Law Act
1977 (pre-1949 enactments) produced the same fine or maximum
fine for different convictions shall be treated for the purpose of this
section as if there were omitted from it so much of it as before 29th
July 1977 had the effect that a person guilty of an offence under it
was liable on summary conviction to a fine or maximum fine less
than the highest fine or maximum fine to which he would have
been liable if his conviction had satisfied the conditions required
for the imposition of the highest fine or maximum fine
Criminal Justice Act 1982, s.38(4)

In these Regulations, unless the context otherwise requires, any
reference to a numbered regulation is a reference to the regulation
bearing that number in these Regulations and any reference in a
regulation to a numbered paragraph is to the paragraph of that
regulation bearing that number
*Education (Individual Pupils' Achievements) (Information) Regulations
1990*

An employer may, in respect of employment for which a particular
poster or leaflet has been approved under para.(4) by displaying
that particular form of poster or giving that particular form of
leaflet and in connection with any such compliance reg.4 shall be
construed as if the references to the approved poster and the
approved leaflet in that regulation were references to the particular
form of poster and the particular form of leaflet approved under
para.(4) and as if the reference in reg.4(3) to revision pursuant to
reg.3(2) were a reference to a revision pursuant to reg.3(5)
*Health and Safety Information for Employees (Modifications and
Repeals) Regulations 1995, Regulation 2(b)(6)*

The Crime (Sentences) Act 1997 Schedule 4, para.5(1)(b) as enacted would have amended the Criminal Justice Act 1967, s.56(2) so as to refer to s.17(3) of the Crime (Sentences) Act 1997. This section would have replaced the Criminal Justice Act 1991, s.40(3) if Chapter 1 of Part 2 of the Crime (Sentences) Act 1997 had been brought into force. The whole of the Chapter (with the exception of s.9) was repealed by the Crime and Disorder Act 1998 Schedule 10 with effect from September 30, 1998. The Crime (Sentences) Act 1997 (Commencement No.2 and Transitional Provisions) Order 1997 brought into force the amendment of the Criminal Justice Act 1967, s.56(2) made by Schedule 4, para.5(1)(b) to the Act and then purported by para.5(3)(b) to amend s.56(2) of the 1967 Act (as so amended) so that the reference to the Crime (Sentences) Act 1997, s.17(3) was replaced by a reference to the Criminal Justice Act 1991, s.40(3). The effect of this amendment would be that the Criminal Justice Act 1967, s.56(2) referred to the Criminal Justice Act, s.40(3) instead of to the Criminal Justice Act 1967, s.62(6): _R. v. Divers_ (1999) 2 Cr. App. Rep. (S) 421 per Klevan, J.

FOLLOW THAT!

SOME AFTER -DINNER STORIES

GETTING UP TO SPEAK

My after-dinner speech was soothing, moving and satisfying. I know this because the audience at first went to sleep, then started walking out, and finally clapped and said, "No More"!

An after-dinner speaker droned on and on, until finally, an exasperated guest approached him with a wine bottle held high above his head. "Don't worry" said the guest to the speaker, "It's not you I'm after. It's the b----r who invited you!"

It may have been the same speaker at a different dinner, but the effect on the guests was exactly the same. Finally in fury a guest threw a bottle which hit, not the speaker, but the chairman sitting next to him. As he sank to the ground the chairman was heard to say, "Hit me again. I can still hear him!"

A famous after-dinner speaker said as he rose to address his audience, holding an old-fashioned microphone in his hand: "At the last dinner I attended and at which I was invited to speak, I spent the entire first course trying to get pepper out of this thing! This speech" he went on, "could have been given by many men, great, fluent, articulate, much more distinguished than I. I don't however see many of them here tonight." As he sat down his next door neighbour tapped him on the leg and said, "Now I'll tell you who is a really good after-dinner speaker."

At a dinner at which F.E. Smith, later Lord Birkenhead, was a guest speaker, things had gone slowly, and several of the speakers had droned on for what seemed like an eternity. Finally, late in the evening, the chairman said, "I am now going to ask Mr Smith to give his address." F.E. rose and said, "My lords, ladies and gentlemen, 32 Grosvenor Square, W1" and sat down!

At a different dinner a speaker was not called on to speak until long after the hour when carriages had been requested. He said only this: "I had two speeches prepared - a long and a short. In view of the late hour I propose to give both. The short one was "Thank you," the long one was "Thank you very much!"

Faced with a similar situation a speaker rose to his feet and said: "This is the only occasion in my life so far that I have been called upon to speak in injury time!"

"I feel rather like Solomon looking at his thousand wives. I know what is expected of me, but I don't know where to begin."

"Ladies and gentlemen," the speaker began, and then said under his breath, "and I think that's a compliment to some of you!"

"Mr Chairman," said the aged speaker, "May I put my glasses on? As one gets older, things get shorter! Not only is it a pleasure and a privilege to be here tonight, it's also extremely inconvenient."

A business man was making an after-dinner speech. Sitting next to him was his wife. When he sat down she leaned towards him and said, "That, darling, was a Rolls-Royce performance - nearly inaudible, well-oiled, and seemed likely to go on for ever!"

A curious, but sometimes very effective way of beginning an after-dinner speech is to use the following pattern:
"The first persons to climb Mount Everest were Edmund Hilary and Sherpa Tensing. If William Pitt had been born 20 years earlier we wouldn't have lost America. Yorkshire pudding tastes just as good with roast lamb as with roast beef. None of this has anything to do with the subject of my talk tonight, but it shows how the mind wanders when you're nervous!"

A judge speaking after dinner said to his audience, "Before I came tonight my host asked me, "Have you tried a rum and pep mixed with a measure of gin and bitters and a large Drambuie?" I replied, "No, but I've tried many a man who has!"

"I apologise for the fact that I have lost my voice. I was speaking last night at the annual dinner of the Scientific and Technical Equipment Development Association and the microphone broke down."

On the morning he was to make an after-dinner speech, the judge said to his wife, "I cut my face. I was concentrating on my speech."

After the speech, as they drove back to their hotel in their limo, his wife said to him, "Pity you didn't concentrate on your face and cut your speech."

The greatest care is required when introducing a speaker, for it is so easy to be misunderstood, and words said in complete innocence can be misconstrued. This was the case when the chairman of a Rotary lunch introduced the speaker by saying, "We are delighted today to welcome Mr Smith. Those of you who have not heard Mr Smith speak before, are eagerly awaiting what he has to say."

The ideal number for a dinner party is two - yourself and the head waiter. But tonight is an exception.

Someone once said to me, and I don't call him a friend, "You do to after-dinner speaking what the Boston strangler did to door-to-door salesmen!"

"The toast which I am proposing is 'Absent Friends'. With this I couple the name of the wine waiter who has not yet managed to get round to this table."

ABOUT JUDGES

An elderly judge walking along Fleet Street towards the Law Courts, approached the traffic lights at Fetter Lane. A huge lorry was stationary at the lights, and as the judge came abreast of the driver, the driver yelled at the judge through his open window, "F---ing Yuppie!" The lights then changed and he put his window up and drove on. The judge's clerk ran up to the judge and said to him, "Blimey, judge! That geezer is out of order driving an artic with eyesight like that."

A bad-tempered lady judge was involved in a protracted argument with a diffident lady barrister in a jury case in the Crown Court. The spat over, the barrister sat down and was handed a note by the foreman of the jury. The judge saw this and asked to see the note, but was assured that it was a personal matter and need not trouble her ladyship. However the judge insisted that she see the note. On it were written the words, "How would you like her for a mother-in-law?"

On a different occasion before the same lady judge, the judge was having a run-in with a senior male counsel. After it was over, counsel said to the judge, "I'm so sorry. I seem to have got across your ladyship," to which the judge replied, "I would never allow counsel to get across me!"

Barrister: (to witness) "Is your appearance here this morning pursuant to a deposition notice which was sent to your solicitor?"
Witness: "No. This is how I dress when I go to work."

Judge: (to defendant) "The charge here is theft of frozen chickens. Are you the defendant?"
Defendant: "No sir. I'm the guy who stole the chickens."

A police officer was giving evidence in the magistrates' court in a case involving the driver of a heavy goods vehicle not displaying obligatory rear lights. The officer described how he followed and stopped the lorry, invited the driver to accompany him to the rear of the vehicle and after caution pointed out that his rear lights were not lit. To which the driver replied, "B----r my rear lights. Where's my f---ing trailer."

In a long trial at the Old Bailey, counsel suggested that Mr Justice Melford Stevenson's recollection of the evidence was incorrect. The shorthand note was read and the judge was right. Counsel apologised. "Don't apologise," said the judge. "It's a long case. Save it all up until the end."

In another case at the Old Bailey, counsel was cross-examining the police officer and asking him why he had made no contemporaneous note. Mr Justice Melford Stevenson crossly rebuked him by saying, "In my years on the Bench I have made a note of no questions and very few answers." To which counsel deferentially replied, "Which no doubt accounts for your lordship's longevity and good humour."

It is reported that Mr Justice Melford Stevenson said to Mr Justice Cooke soon after he had been appointed to the High Court Bench, "Sam, have you got your Archbold?" Cooke J replied, "I'm not sure, but I've got everything Ede and Ravenscroft gave me."

In the Court of Appeal , one of the judges said to counsel, "Mr Y, you say the learned judge did not put this point to the jury, but it was a point you yourself did not take." "Yes" replied counsel, "but it is the learned judge I am criticising, not myself."

In another case in the Court of Appeal, the chairman said to counsel, "Give us some credit for knowing *something*." To this counsel replied, "My lord, that was the mistake I made in the court below."

In a case before the Recorder of London, counsel was taking a witness through his evidence in great detail. When the judge rebuked him he replied, "I must leave no stone unturned in the defence of my client." "But can you not confine yourself to the larger boulders?" asked the judge. "But my Lord," said counsel "your lordship will remember that the giant Goliath was killed by a tiny pebble."

Some academics have been known to express the wish that a suspended sentence were given its medieval meaning.

Mr Justice Gatehouse was heard to say that expert evidence was only an ordinary guess dressed up in evening clothes.

Wilfred Lewis said of the distinguished barrister who appears in court for or in support of the Attorney General (known colloquially as the Treasury devil): "This is an exotic job title for the man who sits behind the Law Officers as they expound the law to the court and then joins (not too obtrusively) in the general merriment."

Gilbert Gray QC used to say that the difference between him and Perry Mason was that Mason examined a witness for three minutes and the witness collapsed. Gray examined a witness for three days and Gray collapsed.

In the witness box at York Crown Court was a small boy. "Do you know what an oath is?", asked the judge in order to help him decide whether he was old enough to be sworn. "Yes" the boy replied, "It's what me dad uses when he falls o'er t'cat."

Judge to defendant, "Why were you not here last Thursday?" "My mum got burnt." "Not badly I hope" said the judge. "Oh yes; good and proper. They don't mess about at Wood Green Crematorium."

Mr Justice Singleton was sitting at Newport Assize, which in days gone by used to have a very small dock. On this occasion the dock was filled with 12 defendants, and because of their numbers, they stood in two rows of six, one row behind the other. The judge entered court and sat down, and the Clerk of Assize rose and whispered to him, "My Lord, the case you have next is a case from Abergavenny. It's a buggery case." "Oh" said the judge, "A buggery case! Let the front row sit down!"

The Bar robing room at the Old Bailey is an unforgiving place, and comments heard there about judges sometimes get uncomfortably near the truth. Among these are reputed to be the following: "There's nothing wrong with Mr Justice A that lockjaw wouldn't cure." And: "Judge M. is improving. Gaps are appearing in his ignorance." And about witnesses: "It's not so much that she's a liar as that she uses the truth sparingly."

Mr Justice Hallett once remarked on the youth of a witness who was a company director. Counsel, Sir Harry Hylton-Foster, replied, "My lord. It's only at the Bar that the plums go to the decrepit."

It was the custom on the North Eastern Circuit (and perhaps on every Circuit) for the Bar to entertain HM judges who were sitting in the area at the time. On one occasion at a Bar Mess at Judges' Night in Leeds, the leader of the Circuit rose to introduce the judges, and began by saying: "Mr Junior! There are judges and judges. Those here tonight are the latter sort!"

Lord Radcliffe told me once of the occasion on which he almost made a mistake.

Judge: "Your face is familiar. Have you been up before me?"
Defendant: "I dunno. What time in the morning does your lordship get out of bed?"

Judge to witness: "Come now. I do want you to be frank."
Witness: "I am being frank. If I was any franker I'd be committing perjury."

A bachelor judge married a lady 50 years younger than him. He consulted a friend concerning the difficulty of such a wide disparity in age, and the friend advised him to arrange for someone to live with them to keep his wife amused. This was done. The friend later asked him how they were, to which the judge replied, "Both pregnant!"

A learned judge opened his daily copy of *The Times*, turned as usual to the obituary page, and read his own obituary. Angry and perplexed, he immediately telephoned his clerk and said, "Percy, have you seen my obituary notice in this morning's newspaper?" "Yes, my lord, I have" said his clerk. "Where is your lordship speaking from?"

A pickpocket's reply to a police officer's inquiry about his occupation: "I'm in the steal business."

An East End market trader was convicted by the magistrates' court of a market offence, and appealed to the local Crown Court. The Notice of Appeal read as follows: "The market notice was not properly conspicuated, so I consolidated a solicitor and he told me it was all a question of the royal provocative."

Late one night a suspect was taken to a police station and was standing outside the interview room. He heard the following conversation from within the room: "What is your name?" Slap ... slap ... slap. "And your address?" Slap ... slap ... slap. "Who are your accomplices?" Slap ... slap ... slap. "Will you please stop hitting me when I am questioning you?"

In the course of an ingenious daylight theft from a furniture store by a thief with a white coat and a pantechnicon, a little old lady came up with a £5 note and asked, "May I pay you my weekly instalment?" to which the reply was, "Not just now, madam, I'm stocktaking."

Counsel to a thief in the witness box charged with stealing clothing: "Mr Smith, isn't your jacket rather too big for you?" "Yes, I know. I must see my tailor about it."

In an indecent assault case in the Crown Court, a female witness was asked to tell the court what the defendant had said to her before the assault. She said she was so embarrassed she would like to write it down. This was done, and the piece of paper was then passed round the jury. The juryman at the end of the back row was asleep, so his neighbour, a lady, nudged him to wake him up, and handed him the note. He read this, turned to her with a surprised look and said, "Wot? Here?"

Judge: "You have been convicted of the abominable crime of buggery, and I sentence you to nine months' imprisonment."
Prison officer to deaf defendant (who had not heard a word): "He says you're an abominable bugger and you're down the nick for nine years."
Judge: "Officer, I echo your sentiments, but you are not allowed to vary my sentences."

F.E. Smith (later Lord Birkenhead) had an infallible way of shutting his opponent up in a final speech. All that he did was to pass his opponent a note on which was written the magic phrase: "Your fly-buttons are undone!"

Advice given by Charles Paley-Scott QC to a barrister who inquired as to the technique of appearing in court before a judge who was slightly deaf: "Boom at him, Bobby. Boom at him!"

In reply to a question from counsel, a witness said, "Bugger all!" The judge, who was slightly hard of hearing said to the clerk of the court "What did the witness say?" "Bugger all, my lord," said the clerk. "That's funny" said the judge, "I distinctly saw his lips move."

A bail application was being made before Mr Ronnie Guest, a London stipendiary magistrate. In the witness box was a police officer describing how he had arrested the defendant caught red-handed in a burglary: "I told the accused that he was under arrest on suspicion of a felony and that I proposed to accompany him to the police station. I told him that he would be charged with an offence under the Theft Act." During this evidence the defendant was bouncing around in the dock, obviously disagreeing. When the officer's evidence was completed, the defendant went into the witness box and said: "What the officer really said was, 'Get your skates on Fred, you've f----d it up this time!'"

A man in a wheelchair claimed exemplary damages against his employer because, so he alleged, he had been crippled for life. After the case, which he won, and as he was wheeled triumphantly out of court, the insurance investigator came up to him and said, "I know you are shamming. You are a fraud and a shyster, and I'm going to follow you for the rest of your life till I prove it!" "In that case," said the man, "I'd better give you next week's itinerary. Tonight I'm staying at the Ritz, tomorrow it's the George V in Paris, and on Thursday I fly to Lourdes for the miracle!"

In the course of a somewhat idiomatic address by counsel the rather elderly judge leaned over to the clerk of the court and said, "Mr Price, hand me up a copy of Sod's Law."

It is not always easy for a judge to take counsel seriously, or perhaps counsel is trying to wind the court up. This was the case when defence counsel said to the judge, "My lord, I am very sorry, my client is unwell, and will not be able to attend court today." "What is the matter with him?" asked the judge. "He fell off the back of a lorry," was the reply.

Judge to barrister: "Your argument is difficult to follow. It's going in one ear and out of the other."
Barrister: "My lord, what is there in between to stop it?"

At the beginning of my career at the bar, I lost a lot of cases I ought to have won. Towards the end I won a lot of cases I ought to have lost. But, overall, justice was done.

Judge's grandchild to grandmother: "Granny, Granny, why are we having jam for tea." "Hush, child. That's because Grandpa has been upheld in the Court of Appeal."

A judge on the Northern Circuit summed up a case of receiving stolen goods in this way: "The first thing which the prosecution have to prove, members of the jury, is that the goods were stolen. The second thing is that the defendant received them. The third thing for the moment escapes me, but let us now deal with the facts."

At Middlesex Quarter Sessions Mr Ewen Montagu QC, the chairman, said to Raphael Tuck, "Mr Tuck, I have the point. Do you think I'm a nitwit?" To this Mr Tuck replied, "My lord, may I take instructions?"

In a different court, Mr Justice Croom-Johnson said to Mr Platts Mills QC, "I have got the point Mr Platts Mills. Do you really think I'm a moron." To this counsel replied, "No, my lord ... No ... moron is not the word I would use to describe your lordship."

In the trial of a charge against a husband for murdering his wife, counsel submitted that there was extreme provocation. "His wife was taunting him with his sexual inadequacy," he said, "an allegation with which your lordship is no doubt all too familiar."

One counsel to another, of a female solicitor: "I say, those are nice legs!" "My mind is on higher things." "They're all right too."

What is the difference between a female barrister and a
rottweiler?
Only the lipstick!

"I have an idea" said the very junior lady barrister to an elderly
silk. "Treat it very gentle", said he. "It's in a very strange place."

AN ODE TO A SHORTHAND WRITER IN A MINI-SKIRT
(with an acknowledgment to Lindsay Bickers)

Juries were often in doubt
As to just what the case was about.
They gazed with delight
At the wonderful sight,
And grudged all the time they were out.

And even some leading QCs
When they heard of the notable knees,
Gave up a good deal
In the Court of Appeal,
And appeared for the minimum fees.

But the chairman, with action reflex,
Showed no interest in matters of sex.
He exclaimed with a snort
"I'll have order in court!
De mini-skirts non curat lex."

In a long and complicated fraud case, the judge summed up at
length, and after he had sent the jury to their room, he retired to
the judges' mess. He there mentioned to one of his brother judges
that he had done the best and most efficacious summing-up of his
whole career. At this point there was a knock on the door and the
lady shorthand-writer appeared. "Judge," she said, "I ought to tell
you that in your summing-up you got the burden of proof wrong.
But it's OK. Don't worry. I'll put it right in the transcript." What the
judge might have told the jury, but hopefully didn't, was the
following: "Members of the jury, if you believe the prosecution you
will find the defendant guilty; if you believe the defence, you will
find him not guilty; if you believe neither, God knows how you'll
find!"

A farm labourer appeared before Mr Justice Elwes charged with an offence of being extremely friendly with a cow. Photographs of the farm were produced and No.24 was a picture of two mournful looking cows in the farmyard. The judge who was a gentleman of great elegance, looked at the photograph and said, "Please help me. Which of the two ladies is the complainant?"

A defendant convicted of an "improper relationship" with a horse was told by the judge in passing sentence that "you need to be in a more stable environment".

Judge: "You have been convicted by this jury of the grievous offence of bigamy. I do not propose to send you to prison. You have acquired not one mother-in-law but two. You have been punished enough."

"I'm a poor man and I want legal aid to help me with my defence," said the defendant in a case in the magistrates' court. "What is the charge?" asked the chairman. The clerk replied, "The charge is making a false statement for the purpose of obtaining legal aid."

A defendant was asked by the judge if he would like legal aid. "No my lord," said he, "I would rather defend myself. This is a serious charge."

Prisoner to judge: "May I have legal aid? I usually do."

Counsel to judge: "My client applies for legal aid on two grounds; one, he is not very bright, and two, he is employed on important government work."

A defendant stood in the dock on an indictment containing two counts of armed robbery, both on the same day. The judge explained how serious the charges were and as he had no counsel, suggested that he should have legal aid to pay for a barrister to represent him. The defendant refused, emphatically and repeatedly. The case began, prosecution witness after prosecution witness was called, no questions were asked of them by the defendant, the jury retired and very soon returned with an expected verdict of guilty on both counts. Before passing sentence the judge asked the defendant if he had anything to say, to which he replied, "I can't have done it because on that day I was in the nick - in the Scrubs - banged up." "Why on earth did you not tell the jury this earlier?" asked the judge. "Because it might have prejudiced my defence," replied the defendant.

Plaintiff's solicitor: "What doctor treated you for the injuries you sustained while at work?"
Plaintiff: "Dr Smith."
Plaintiff's solicitor: "And what kind of physician is Dr Smith?"
Plaintiff: "Well, I'm not sure, but you said he was a good plaintiff's doctor."

Lawyer in a US court to prospective juror: "How do you feel about defence attorneys?"
Juror: "I think they should all be drowned at birth."
Lawyer: "Well then obviously you are biased for the prosecution."
Juror: "That's not true. I think prosecutors should be drowned at birth too."

Judge: "I know you, don't I?"
Defendant: "Uh, yes."
Judge: "All right, tell me, how do I know you?"
Defendant: "Your Honour, do I have to tell you?"
Judge: "Of course. If you don't, you might be guilty of obstructing the course of public justice."
Defendant: "Okay. I was your bookie."

Mr Justice Gould was trying a case at York Assizes and after the case had been proceeding for a couple of hours he noticed that there were only 11 jurors in the jury-box. "Where," he demanded, "is the twelfth?" "May it please you, my lord," said one of the 11, "he has gone away about some other business, but he has left his verdict with me."

The art of court reporting is clearly in decline. The following relentlessly logical piece of prose appeared in the *Sunday Strand* for 1900: "A man killed a dog belonging to another man. The son of the man whose dog was killed proceeded to whip the man who killed the dog of the man he was the son of. The man who was the son of the man whose dog was killed, was arrested on a complaint of the man who was assaulted by the son of the man whose dog the man who was assaulted had killed."

In an appeal case in the Court of Criminal Appeal (as it then was) with the irascible Lord Goddard, Lord Chief Justice, in the chair, counsel was addressing the court and used the phrase "My lord, I humbly submit that ..." Lord Goddard interrupted him to say, "Humbly submit! Humbly submit! I never humbly submitted to anyone in my whole life." Another counsel, in a stage whisper, said behind his hand, "You could have fooled me!"

Mr Justice Goddard (as he then was) sentenced a defendant to a long term of years and when he ordered that the man be taken below, the defendant shouted, "You're a nasty old bugger." The case went to appeal and the appeal was dismissed, but at the end of his judgment Lord Justice Swift said this: "According to the shorthand note, the prisoner passed an observation about the habits of our brother Goddard which, so far as this court is aware, is entirely without foundation."

Mr Justice Ashworth was trying a case in the Assize Court when proceedings were interrupted by the loud noise of a pile-driver being operated nearby. "What is that noise?", asked the judge. Defence counsel in a stage whisper said, "The noise of the police obtaining another voluntary confession."

In opening a rape case before Mr Justice Goddard, counsel said, "My lord this incident took place in a crowded restaurant." The judge interrupted and said, "In my experience an incident like this usually happens when a restaurant is closed." Counsel replied, "My lord, I haven't had that experience!"

An action was being heard at Leeds Assizes. It was a case brought by a man with a paralysed left arm. Counsel on his behalf claimed that he could never work again. The judge said, "He's an intelligent man. If he works hard he might even become a High Court Judge." Counsel for the defendant whispered, "He's not as paralytic as all that!"

In a criminal case before Mr Justice Thompson the defendant was charged with a serious offence of indecency. He also had a hacking cough. The judge said to counsel, "Mr A, would your client like to suck a Fisherman's Friend?" "No thank you my lord," said counsel, "he's in enough trouble as it is."

Judges at the Old Bailey are properly addressed as "Your Lordship". Defendants from foreign parts occasionally get it wrong and use phrases such as "Your Excellency", "Your Highness" or "Your Majesty". One such defendant got it very wrong and addressed the judge as "O Lord Most High"!

An English judge, lecturing to law students in Los Angeles, said, "In order to succeed at the Bar you need three things ..." A male student was heard to say "If I had three things I'd be in a circus."

It is often said that a trial judge must be quick, courteous and wrong. This, however, does not mean that the Court of Appeal should be slow, rude and right, for that would be to usurp the function of the House of Lords.

Applicants for circuit judgeships sometimes invite their influential friends to write letters of commendation to the Lord Chancellor's department. One such letter read as follows: "This man would make no more than a very average judge." When the Lord Chancellor read this he remarked, "Appoint him! We need a few very average judges!"

It is (or used to be) the custom on the North Eastern Circuit that a member of the Bar who was elected to become a member of the Circuit Bar Mess, had to make a speech "stating his or her pretensions." A lady barrister stated her pretensions in this very unusual and indeed memorable way:

> "To speak without fee
> Is obnoxious to me
> So I'm afraid
> Until I am paid,
> Not a word will be heard
> From this newly called bird."

In a case at York Assizes, the judge was about to pass sentence on a defendant who had been convicted and who was standing in the dock, and asked him what his employment was. The defendant was very deaf. He obviously misheard as his reply was, "I have a wife and nine children". The question was repeated, but he gave the same reply, "I have a wife and nine children." The judge then asked the prison officer standing next to him to help. The prison officer shouted into his ear, "He means what do you do in the daytime."

Lord Birkett, when addressing the Ellesmere Society at Oxford, described how he had been defending a pickpocket on Assize and succeeded in persuading the jury to acquit his client. He was sitting in his railway carriage to go back to London when he was surprised and perhaps a little mortified to see his client come and sit down in the seat opposite. "Can you tell me the time please?" asked the client. Just in time Birkett recalled the nature of the client's offence. "Sorry," he said, "I don't have my watch with me." "I'll just slip out and get you one," was the quick rejoinder.

Lord Denning used to tell how the jury acquitted the defendant in the first criminal case he summed up, on a charge of driving under the influence of drink. The next case was a burglary case, and the alleged burglar had been arrested at the door of the house complete with a full housebreaker's kit. In his summing-up Mr Justice Denning (as he then was) said to the jury, "If you think that at dead of night in a darkened house this defendant had come along out of the kindness of his heart to make a gift of his jemmies, his screwdrivers, his case-opener and his gloves to the householder, you will of course acquit him." They did!

Mr Justice Avory once said, "Any fool like Branson or Horridge can get a guilty man convicted. It takes a chap like Travers Humphreys or me to stop the innocent getting away unscathed!"

A good moral for judges is never to try to prompt a witness. This is illustrated by a case at Cardiff Assizes where the charge was one of indecent exposure. A female witness described how the defendant undid his trousers. There was then a long pause, and the judge, trying to make her feel more comfortable and less embarrassed, suggested, "Did he then take out his organ?" The witness replied, "Looked more like a penny whistle to me!"

Young police officers receive training at the Metropolitan Police College, and in the course of a rigorous training they are given certain tests. One such test was as follows:
"You are on patrol in an outer London borough when an explosion occurs in a gas main in a nearby street. On investigation you find that a large hole has been blown in the footpath and there is an overturned van lying nearby. Inside the van there is a strong smell of alcohol. Both occupants - a man and a woman - are injured. You recognise the man, who is in the driving seat, as a disqualified driver, and the woman as the wife of your Divisional Inspector, who is at present away at the Police College. A passing motorist stops to offer you assistance and you recognise him as a man who is wanted

for armed robbery. Suddenly a man runs out of a nearby house, shouting that his wife is expecting a baby and that the shock of the explosion has made the birth imminent. At that moment you notice that a man is crying for help, having been blown into an adjacent canal by the explosion. He cannot swim. In addition there are two dogs fighting in the street. Neither is wearing a collar. A group of men is standing in the door of a nearby public house, drinking after hours, and shouting encouragement to the dogs, urging them to fight. Bearing in mind the provisions of the Mental Health Act, describe in a few words what actions you would take."
One of the bright young officers thought for a moment, picked up his pen and wrote: "Remove uniform and mingle with crowd."

Compensation - it is widespread on both sides of the Atlantic and everyone has heard of the burglar who in the course of breaking into a house was injured when he fell through a skylight and added insult to injury by suing the householder for having unsafe premises. But not everyone has heard of the case in a US District Court in 1971 where a plaintiff brought proceedings against Satan for causing the plaintiff misfortune and misery, thereby violating his constitutional rights. The judge dismissed the case because "the complaint contains no allegation of residence by the defendant in this district" and "the plaintiff has failed to include with his complaint the required form of instructions for the United States Marshal for directions as to service of process."

At the West Riding Quarter Sessions in October 1940 a defendant failed to appear at court. The chairman inquired why, and counsel replied, "He is a reservist and has been called to the colours and is now in Egypt." "What is the charge?" asked the chairman. "Stealing six hens," was the reply. "Leave him where he is", said the chairman, "He has the makings of an excellent batman."

Mr Justice Fisher was hearing a claim by a miner against the National Coal Board. In the course of the case he went for a view and travelled to the coal face on a conveyor belt. At the end of the journey he said to the Mine Manager, "It was a curious ride. It was exactly like being stimulated sexually by a belly dancer!" The manager replied, "Your lordship has the advantage of me there!"

A judge and his family were travelling along a motorway in the family car pulling a trailer. Inadvertently the speed limit was exceeded, and the car was stopped by a police car, and pulled on to the hard shoulder. The police officer walked back to the driver's door and informed the judge that he had been exceeding the speed limit and cautioned him. He then took down full particulars in his notebook. His last question was, "What's your occupation?" "Judge" was the reply. The officer closed his notebook and walked back to his car. Half way there he stopped, scratched his head, and walked back to the judge's car. "You mean flower-show judge?" he said.

Mr Justice Cassels to rather long-winded counsel, "Mr C. Can you tell me quite shortly, are you in the next case?" A mirror image of this request was a question which counsel, perhaps with good reason, addressed to Mr Justice Hallett: "My Lord, could your lordship give us some idea as to how long this case will last?"

An Irish counsel, Mr M, on the Northern Circuit, was instructed in a civil case, and was reading to the judge a long reported judgment in a previous case in the Court of Appeal upon which he strongly relied. At the end of his submission he handed the report up to the judge, who looked at what counsel had been reading, and said,"But Mr M , this is the dissenting judgment." "Yes, my lord," was the reply, "But that is the judgment I prefer."

The same counsel was appearing before Judge Peel in the County Court in a claim by his client for the recovery of £30 as money had and received. A great deal turned on the credibility of the plaintiff who had given evidence. Mr M reviewed the facts and then said, "My client's evidence in my submission should be accepted. Does your Honour think that he would perjure his immortal soul for the sum of £30?" "Mr M," said the judge, "what price had you in mind?"

Nervous counsel was appearing before Sir Anthony Hawke at the Old Bailey on behalf of a defendant called Mrs Winterbottom who earned her living by taking in washing. Unhappily when he rose to introduce himself to the judge he became a little confused and said, "My Lord I appear for Mrs Winterwoman, a washerbottom." "Just so, Mr H," said the judge, "A glum name for an even glummer occupation."

Lord Birkett once said at a large evening gathering, "The speech I'm making tonight is one I have already made twice - once at Dartmoor and once at the Law Society. I must apologise to anyone here tonight who has heard it before."

Harold Macmillan, after he ceased to be Prime Minister, was invited by the Sheriffs to lunch at the Old Bailey with the judges. After lunch he made a short informal speech in the course of which he said that his wife said to him when he left home that morning, "Can you find your way to the Old Bailey?" He replied, "I can find my way there all right, but I'm not sure if I can find my way back!"

Lord Justice Tasker Watkins, VC, was one of the many distinguished advocates of the Wales and Chester Circuit. He had also been decorated for conspicuous bravery in action during the Second War. There was an occasion at the Swansea Assizes when he was still in practice at the Bar when he was observed by the judge to have been sitting in court for some time, although not involved in the case which was being heard. "Mr Watkins," said the judge, "I see you in court. Is there anything which I can do to help?" "My lord," said counsel, "I am in the next case." "Why did you not ask me earlier to release you?" "My lord," said Tasker, "I did not have the courage!"

In a civil case at Leeds Assizes, Mr Justice Rigby Swift, who was noted for his Northern directness, was being addressed at inordinate length by counsel for the plaintiff (as the claimant in those days was called). Counsel for the defendant passed him a note. This the judge observed and asked to see the note. Counsel objected, as he submitted that it was a personal matter, but objections were over-ruled and the judge saw the note, which read: "Why don't you sit down? Can't you see the old b---- is with you?" "Mr Smith, have you read this note?" asked the judge of counsel for the plaintiff. "My lord, yes I have," said he with considerable apprehension. "Well, Mr Smith," said the judge, "Read it again!"

On a different occasion, when Mr Justice Rigby Swift was sitting as a red judge at the Old Bailey, a witness in the witness box said, "May the Lord strike me dead if I am not telling the truth!" The judge said, "You must not say that. We don't want any tragedies here!"

A very long-winded counsel was appearing before Lord Chief Justice Coleridge, and was apologising to the learned judge for taking so much time in his address. "Time?" replied Coleridge CJ, "Time, Mr Smithers! You have encroached upon eternity!"

In a different court on a later date, the same counsel was again addressing the court at length. "I'm sorry, my lord," he said, "I may have said that before." "I shouldn't worry, Mr Smithers," said the judge, "it was a very long time ago!"

Earlier in the same Assize, Mr Justice Rigby Swift had upbraided counsel Dermot McKee for speaking too quietly. Counsel then took great care to enunciate with great clarity, and at the end of the case the judge said, "Mr McIver (*sic*) I congratulate you. I heard every word you said. Yes, you'd make a very good supporter for a football team."

A barrister is someone who knows practically nothing about practically everything. And they don't change their spots when they become judges.

It is said in the United States that if the District Attorney is strong on his law he shouts about the law; if he's strong on his facts he shouts about the facts; if he's weak on both he shouts louder.

Typing errors can occur to anyone and at any time, even to solicitors in their instructions to counsel. This was the case in a set of instructions sent to counsel in an Admiralty case. These read as follows: "The *Mary Jane* was lying in London River. She developed a strong lust to port."

Lord Reid was once asked whether he ever read the papers before he went into court. He replied, "No. I don't want to get any preconceived ideas." Lord Wilberforce, when asked the same question, replied, "I always do. It is essential that someone should have preconceived ideas."

The practice used to be that judges walked from the High Court to Lincoln's Inn and back at lunch-time, wearing their top hats. On one occasion Mr Justice Goff, walking top-hatted through New Square, was seen by a Cockney builder. "Gor!" he said, "Look at 'im, e's lost 'is 'earse."

Judges should always, when passing sentence, remember the possibility of being reported in *Private Eye*. This of course would not have applied many years ago to Mr Justice Maule, who said to a teenager convicted of assaulting a young girl by placing his hand on her private parts, "Next time, young man, you will go inside!" It might not even have applied to Judge John Maude who said in his sentencing remarks on two men charged and convicted of an act of gross indecency, "You men must pull yourselves together!"

Defendant: "My defence is that I were drunk. Drunk as a judge!"
Judge: "Don't you mean 'drunk as a lord'?"
Defendant: "Yes, m'lord."

The defendant was a building contractor's foreman of a mountainous physique. Having received his wages for a week's work, he went on a drinking spree at a Kilburn public house, and then broke the jaw of a man with whom he got into an argument. He had 30 previous convictions for being drunk and incapable or drunk and disorderly, almost all of these incidents taking place on a pay day. He appeared before Judge Maude at the Old Bailey, pleaded guilty to a serious assault, and was sentenced by the learned judge in these terms: "Your learned counsel has satisfied me that you have an unusual drink problem. You get drunk on pay days. I have decided not to send you to prison if you will give me your solemn promise that on pay days you will not drink any alcohol, not even a teeny weeny sherry."

The speech in mitigation of counsel in the case of a man charged with murder, but convicted of manslaughter of both his parents, was brief and to the point. "My lord, my client is an orphan!"

English law, people say, is a creature of precedent. The art of court reporting is therefore very important, and we currently have a limited number of excellent law reports. In former times, however, things were different, and each individual shorthand-writer published his own set of law reports, entitled with his own name. One famous nineteenth century reporter was Mr Cox. This explains the following interlude at Inner London Quarter Sessions, when Christmas Humphries QC was addressing the then chairman, Mr R.E. Seaton:
Humphries: "Has your lordship got 3 Cox?"
Seaton: "No, Mr Humphries, no, but I'll get along."

Counsel, pompously, to witness: "Did you see the shemozzle?" No answer. "Did you see the melée?" No answer. "Did you see the fracas?" No answer. "Try him in English, Mr Smith," said the judge to counsel, and to the witness, "Did you see the fight, sir?" The witness replied, "I saw everything."

In the same case counsel said to the judge in the course of his argument, "Does your lordship follow me?" To this the judge replied, "Yes, Mr Smith, I am following you closely, but where are you going?"

The Recorder of London was addressing the boys of a City school at Speech Day. Before his speech one of the boys approached him and asked for his autograph. After he had spoken, the same boy approached him again and asked whether he could have four more of his autographs. When asked why he wanted them he said, "Well, I've just discovered I can swap five of yours for one of Mrs Thatcher."

Barristers never get past it, they just lose their appeal.

Notes on pieces of scrap paper sometimes left behind in jury retiring rooms, and collected and destroyed at the conclusion of the case by the jury bailiffs, occasionally give a clue to the reason for the jury's decision and throw a glimmer of light on the confidential darkness which blankets their deliberations. One such note read: "Are we agreed the defendant did it? Yes. Are we agreed the judge was a s..t? Yes. Are we agreed we let the defendant off? Yes." In this story lies, perhaps, a moral for judges.

The perpetual complaint of progressive law students seems to be: "Our judges are not only not with it - they are without it. They are so full of themselves they throw away the letters and keep the envelopes."

Ron Jacobs once said that he had a lot of friends who were practising lawyers, but that he wished they would stop practising and get on with it!

Do not suppose that Her Majesty's judges finish work at 4.30 pm. They have all sorts of things to do after that - golf, tennis, bridge!

A red judge, sitting at the Old Bailey, was rather puzzled as to what would be an appropriate sentence in the sex case he was trying, so at the end of the day he popped along to see the Lord Chief Justice. "What should one give a man who allows himself to be buggered?" he asked. The Lord Chief Justice, whose mind was on his own case, replied: "Oh, a couple of quid or whatever you happen to have in your pocket."

Lawyers love semantics, people say, and argue endlessly about the meaning of words. A word which occasions constant argument is the word "inference". On the meaning of this word William Hungate, a former Democratic congressman from Missouri, had this to say: "If some guy brought an elephant through that door some doubters would say, 'It is an inference that it's an elephant. It could be a mouse with a glandular condition'."

Circumstantial evidence raises an inference of guilt. If, to take an example once suggested by Judge Blagden, the evidence against a defendant on a charge of driving under the influence of drink was that he was seen licking his lips when leaving a public house the inference might be that he had had a drink. It might equally be that he had been kissing the barmaid. An unopened bottle of whisky found on the back seat of his car raised no inference at all - an unopened bottle (it could be said) had never done anyone any harm - nor any good either.

In a case in the Crown Court, counsel's instructing solicitor appeared in court behind him in a low-cut dress which became, day by day, more and more revealing. After the case was over, the judge happened to be sitting at dinner next to counsel and said to him. "I saw you in court in that recent case sitting in front of your soliciting instructor."

Politicians, like judges, approach every problem with an open mouth.

Three retired judges were sitting in their club. One said, "I used to read Shakespeare's plays in the folio edition, but now it's difficult because my eyesight is so bad." The second said, "I used to listen to Mozart's concertos, but it's now difficult as my hearing is so bad." The third said, "Last night I said to my wife, "We must have sex." She replied, "We had it half an hour ago." It's all very difficult. My memory is so bad!

A father lay on his death-bed, surrounded by his family - his wife and three sons. The eldest son was President of the Law Society, the second son was a High Court judge, the youngest was a spendthrift and a drop-out. "Am I really the father of our youngest son," he breathed to his wife. "Yes," said she, and her husband died. "What a good thing," she said to her friend later, "He didn't ask me who was the father of the elder two."

In the expansive days of the 1920s, Sir Felix Cassel, a Bencher of Lincoln's Inn, was being driven home after a Grand Night in the Inn by his chauffeur in his large and elegant motor car. Half way home, descending a long hill, the chauffeur said, "Sir Felix, the brakes have failed!" With great presence of mind, Sir Felix replied, "Well, James, be sure to hit something cheap!"

A balding chancery judge, whose customary hairdresser practised in a shop in Chancery Lane, complained to the hairdresser that, although he had so little hair, they still charged him the full price. The hairdresser (who knew a thing or two about the law) said, "Yes, judge, but in your case we have to charge a search fee!"

Judge Alan Trapnell used to say towards the end of his career that he was getting to an age when temptation was more difficult to find than to resist! Seventy was a good age in his view. When a woman said yes he was flattered, when she said no he was relieved.

It is said by property lawyers that the shortest letter in the world was written by a tenant who had been given a peremptory notice to quit by his landlord. The letter read: "Dear Sir, I remain, Yours faithfully."

One should always remember Shakespeare's phrase (Edgar, "King Lear" Act II, Scene 4) "Keep thy foot out of brothels." An individual who forgot this was a High Court judge sitting at Nottingham Assize many years ago. One evening after court he visited a brothel in Low Pavement in order to enjoy the company of Annie Spraggs. In the course of his enjoyment he sadly expired. The lady made the fatal mistake of ringing the police instead of ringing his clerk at the judges' lodgings. The matter therefore became public, and an inquest was held. When giving evidence at the inquest Annie Spraggs said, "The old gentleman gave a grunt, and I thought he'd come, but he'd gone."

It is inadvisable to be rude to a judge in public; to do so risks punishment for contempt of court. An aggrieved defendant in the County Court was lucky. He threw a dead cat at the judge and the judge said, "If you do that again I shall send you to prison!" Perhaps luckiest of all was the Australian solicitor who, when served with an injunction remarked, "Justice Beach has got his hand on his dick". When told of this, the judge held the solicitor to be in contempt. The matter was appealed to the Supreme Court of Victoria, where Justice Cummins held that the words used amounted to calling the trial judge a wanker. "It may be offensive" he said, "but it is not a contempt of court for a person to describe a judge as a wanker. These words do not undermine confidence in the administration of justice. They undermine confidence in the persona of the solicitor who spoke them."

While sitting at Winchester Assizes, Mr Justice Lawson travelled to and from the judges' lodgings in the judicial Rolls-Royce. One day, returning to the court after lunch, a man in the street gave the Rolls-Royce the two-finger sign. He was at once arrested, brought before the court and arraigned for contempt. In his defence he said, "I thought it was the Lord Mayor."

In a case before the Recorder of London, Sir James Miskin, at the Old Bailey, a youth was standing in the witness box with his hands in his pockets, apparently chewing gum. "Are you masticating?" asked the judge. "No guvn'nor, I'm not," said the young man, removing his hands from his pockets with great speed, but continuing to chew gum.

"I used to come to the Royal Courts of Justice for justice, but I have come away so many times empty-handed that I now just come for the money."

According to a distinguished Georgia judge, "An appellate judge in the cool of the evening undoes what a better man did in the heat of the day."

A newly qualified solicitor applied to a large City firm of solicitors for his first job and was called for an interview in front of the partners. They seemed to him to show a certain lack of enthusiasm for him, and he asked them why. He was told it was his beard. He at once offered to shave it off, but the senior partner said: "Mr Richards, you don't seem to understand. It's not that we will not take anyone with a beard. The position is that we will not take anyone who ever has had a beard."

Judge to defendant (in US Court): "You are charged with habitual drunkenness. Have you anything to say in your defence?"
Defendant: "Your Honour, habitual thirstiness."

A City solicitor appeared at the pearly gates and asked for admission. St Peter came forward and said, "You are the first City solicitor we have had here, and the oldest. You are 150 years old." "No, I'm not," said the solicitor, "I'm 75." "Sorry," said St Peter, "I added up the hours of work you had claimed in your bills of costs!"

Santa Claus, a cheap solicitor and an expensive solicitor are walking together along Fleet Street when suddenly a £50 note blows across the pavement. Which one of the three picks it up? The answer is the expensive solicitor; the other two are figments of the imagination.

Mr Justice Veale recounted how at an official dinner which he attended while on Assize, all the menu cards bore the picture of a different tropical bird. The card before the judge displayed a certain lack of tact. It had a picture of a red-bellied parrot, and the description of the bird included the phrases, "This bird moves from place to place according to season. It can be tamed and makes a charming pet, but it only learns to speak a few sentences."

Defendant (in US Court): "Judge, I want you to appoint me another lawyer."
Judge: "And why is that?"
Defendant: "Because the Public Defender isn't interested in my case."
Judge (to Public Defender): Do you have any comments on the defendant's motion?"
Public Defender: "I'm sorry, your Honour, I wasn't listening."

A witness in a case before a slightly pompous judge gave his name as Malumbo Karimba Okusi. The judge asked him. "Tell me. Is there an apostrophe after the O in your surname?" When he was told there was not, he commented, "We can therefore take it, can we, that you do not come from Ireland?"

Many barristers are as good at relaxing as they are in court. This is certainly true of Oliver Gogarty, an Irish barrister, who, after a heavy night out, was put on the Dublin train by his colleagues, rather the worse for wear. He was seen to open the door and put his shoes out (to be cleaned) as the train moved off.

Some counsel are masters of the art of two-edged compliments. Or perhaps it is that they don't realise quite what they've said. This was the case where a young barrister, having been corrected by the judge, accepted the correction in these terms: "Your lordship is right, and I am wrong, as your lordship usually is."

How not to be courteous: "I bow to your lordship's superior ignorance!"

Court clerk to counsel: "His lordship is not well today."
Counsel: "Nothing trivial I hope."

A law student was asked the difference between a mortgagor and a mortgagee. His reply was, "Since the Sex Disqualification (Removal) Act, there is no difference."

Gilbert Gray, QC, tells how he had made his mind up to be a Methodist Minister, but decided that the money wasn't everything and went to the Bar instead.

Counsel: "My lord, this is an appeal against the refusal of the Kingston magistrates to grant my client an affiliation order in bastardy. We appeal because she was wickedly wronged by the man at the back of the court."
Judge: "Mr Smith, on what ground?"
Counsel: "My lord, on the Richmond Athletic Ground."

Judge to counsel: "I must apologise to counsel. I shall not be able to deliver my judgment as I have left the draft at my house in the country."
Counsel: "My lord, fax it up."
Judge: "Yes, it does rather."

An elderly lady with a progressive streak had a fondness for fast cars, and one day on the motorway was exceeding the speed limit, when she noticed a police car behind her. She accelerated to get away, and pulled in to the next service area well ahead of the police, quickly parked her car, and dashed into the ladies' lavatories. Twenty minutes later, when she emerged, two police officers were at the entrance, arms akimbo, waiting for her. Totally unabashed, she said to them, "I bet you thought I'd never make it!"

Leading counsel was staying recently in a room in a hotel of the town where he was appearing and he happened to pick up the Bible placed in the room by the Gideons. Opening the book, he found written on the flyleaf in beautiful Gothic script these words: "Despite ravaging inflation, the wages of sin remain the same."

A prison governor was asked to write a report on a prisoner who was shortly to be released. The report read: "X is studying to become a member of the criminal Bar. His cunning ensures his success. If only he can develop an evil temper he will make an admirable judge."

Two prisoners were walking round the exercise yard of Lewes Prison. One said to the other, "How long are you in for?" Pause. "14 days" was the reply. Pause. "What for?" Pause. "I stole a row of lettuces." Pause. "How long are you in for?" Pause. "5 years." Pause. "What was that for?" Pause. "Rape" was the answer. Long Pause. "Blimey! Did you steal the whole field?!"

Three men met by chance on a long train journey, and got into conversation. One said, "My son is 23 and he has just started at the Bar." The second said, "My son is 30 and he has just been made a surgical registrar." The third said, "My son is 16 and he is helping the police with their enquiries."

Three young ladies were called up for interview for a job in barristers' chambers. "Consider this problem," said the head of chambers. "You are shipwrecked on a desert island with 40 men. One of the men makes an indecent approach to you?" The first lady said, "I'd swim for it." The second said, "I would seek protection." The third said, "What's the problem?"

A London solicitor was visiting the headquarters of the European Union on behalf of a client. When he returned he was asked how he got on, his opposite number, the French solicitor, being a woman. "She found my accent so amusing she nearly fell out of bed," he replied.

A visitor to the Isle of Alderney asked, "Is it right that you only appear in court here on a drunk driving charge if you hit another vehicle?" "Gracious, no," was the reply, "the other vehicle has to be stationary!"

In the words of Serjeant Arabin, "If ever there was a clearer case than this case of two persons acting together then that case is this case."

A letter received by a Manchester firm of solicitors from a client read: "I am afraid that I could not keep my appointment as I have been poorly with piles and I am behind with my work which is piling up."

A middle-aged man was knocked to the ground in a shopping centre by a group of young thugs who stole his wallet. As he lay on the ground he was passed and ignored by many members of the public, until at last a young lady came up, knelt beside him and asked what happened. He told her and she said, "Oh, I must go after them at once and see if I can help them. I am a social worker."

ABOUT JURIES

In a case at York Quarter Sessions, the jury were sworn, and the case was about to begin when one of the jurors stood up and asked the judge if he could ask a question. He was told he could. His question was, "Sir, if I die will my son inherit my seat?"

In a short criminal case the judge sent the jury to their room, and after three hours called them back into court. "You are obviously having difficulty in reaching a verdict." A juryman got up and said, "We haven't got as far as the verdict yet. We still haven't agreed on our foreman."

It is said that juries are a mirror image of the society in which they live. In a case at West Ham Quarter Sessions a jury was selected and asked to wait at the back of the court while another matter was cleared up. The judge then invited them to "take their rightful place." To a man they then all climbed into the dock.

In a case where the evidence for the prosecution was very strong, the jury retired and elected their foreman, who immediately took a poll as to their verdict. The result was, 11 for guilty, one for not guilty. The foreman asked the dissenting member why he dissented, and his reply was, "They've wasted our time. Now we're going to waste some of theirs."

A jury in a plain case took two hours to reach their verdict. Counsel happened a short time later to be having tea in a café near the court, and was sitting next to one of the jurors in the case. "We were surprised you took so long to reach a verdict," he said. "Oh," said the juryman, "We reached our verdict in 10 minutes. We spent the rest of the time arguing on how much we should tip the usher."

Judges should never assume that their directions to a jury go unheeded. In a case at a London court, the judge took a favourable view of the defence case and said to the jury in the course of his summing-up: "Members of the jury, you may think that this case is a storm in a teacup." Later, when the jury returned to court, the clerk of the court asked them, "How do you find the defendant, guilty or not guilty?" The foreman replied: "We find this is a storm in a teacup."

Juries sometimes fail to grasp the essential point. For example in a case of driving while under the influence of drink at Mold Quarter Sessions, the chairman summed the case up and sent the jury out to consider their verdict. After two hours they came back with a note saying: "Was it raining at the time?"

A murder trial was taking place in a court in the USA. The defence were relying on the fact that no body had been found, and therefore it was impossible to be sure that the victim was dead. The defence attorney said to the jury, "I'm going to ask that the door at the back of the court be opened, and for all you know the person

the prosecution say is dead may be standing there alive and well."
The door was then opened and the jury looked round. There was
no sign of the victim. The attorney invited the jury to acquit, since
he submitted the fact that they looked at the door proved that they
were not sure the victim was dead. The jury retired and convicted
in 20 minutes. "How could you?" said the attorney to one member
as they left the court. "We all looked at the door," said the juror,
"and so did everyone else. The only guy who didn't was the
defendant."

The scene is South Africa. In a criminal case there before Judge
Greenberg, the evidence against the defendant was overwhelming.
The judge summed the case up and sent the jury to their room,
expecting that they would return in a few minutes with an
appropriate guilty verdict. The hours went by, and eventually the
jury returned and were asked if they had agreed on their verdict
and what their verdict was. "Not guilty!" said the foreman. "Not
guilty!" said the judge. "On what grounds?" "Insanity," said the
foreman. "What! All 12 of you?" said the judge.

In an armed robbery case the jury were sent to their room and were
in retirement for three hours. They then came back to court to ask
the judge to remind them of the evidence of a vitally important
eye-witness. The judge did so. As they were leaving the jury box to
return to their private room, the defendant said to his solicitor in
a voice unfortunately loud enough for the last juror to hear, "I
knew it. I should have shot her."

A judge was summing up to the jury in a case of public nuisance,
and at the end of his charge he invited the jury to retire to consider
their verdict. At this point the foreman stood up and said, "We are
grateful to your lordship. Until we heard your lordship we had no
idea what a public nuisance was."

"When I sum a case up to a jury," said the judge to a friend, "I do it down the middle, being neither partial nor impartial."

A juror in Mr Justice Cassel's court asked to be excused from jury service. When asked for the reason he replied, "My wife is about to conceive." "Do you not mean that she is about to be confined?" said the judge, "But never mind. Whichever it is, you have obviously got to be there!"

It is an article of faith among counsel at the Old Bailey that if the man who is elected foreman of the jury has a beard, and affirms instead of taking the oath, the odds are 9 to 1 that the jury will acquit. If he has a copy of *The Guardian* in his pocket, it's a dead cert.

A court of law is a frightening place, and sometimes witnesses under stress get muddled when they have to take the oath. This happened to a dentist who went into the witness box and swore that his evidence would be "the tooth, the whole tooth and nothing but the tooth".

A State judge in Arkansas was once heard to say, "As long as I am sitting on this Bench every woman in this town can walk the streets in safety."

ABOUT MAGISTRATES

Counsel, pompously, in a case before a stipendiary magistrate: "My client approached the cross-roads, looked to right and left, but at the moment critique he was struck by the other motor car which he never saw. I put in his licence - it is a virgin." The stipendiary, addressing the defending motorist said, "You must have realised that when a virgin approaches the moment critique it is incumbent on her to proceed with especial care."

It is said that at one time there was a sticker in front of counsel's seats in the Chief Metropolitan Magistrate's Court at Bow Street which read: "Please do not ask for bail, as a refusal often offends."

The charge was a criminal charge before a stipendiary magistrate, and the female defendant had pleaded guilty. The magistrate said, "You are fined £20." The defendant said, "I'll pay on Thursday." The magistrate said, rebuking her for her discourtesy, "If I *may* I'll pay on Thursday." "Oh no," said the defendant. "I don't want you to pay the fine. I'll pay it myself."

Chairman of a lay bench, sentencing a man convicted of indecent exposure: "We have carefully considered sending you to prison, but we propose to make you feel it in your pocket." On a different occasion the same chairman said, at the end of the evidence, "We find the case proved, and you are fined £50, but if we were sure about it you would have got much more."

A woman shoplifter before lay magistrates was remanded for a psychiatric report. In due course she returned for a resumed hearing and was asked by the chairman what the psychiatrist had told her. "Take things more quietly," was her reply.

Magistrate to defendant motorist: "Are you saying you collided with a stationary bollard?"
Defending solicitor to magistrate: "I can't recall seeing many ambulant bollards."
Magistrate: "Perhaps only after closing time!"

Chairman of magistrates' court: "We've had considerable doubts about this case and we don't propose to give you the benefit of any of them."

Defendant to elderly solicitor: "And how shall I give my evidence?"

Solicitor: "Oh, just let it come out as though it were the truth."

Geoffrey Lane QC (later Lord Chief Justice) appeared at the Scunthorpe magistrates' court, and in the course of his argument, quoted a leading case on the point he was developing. The chairman stopped him and said, "Now then young man, we had that case for breakfast." Later counsel asked a question of a witness in the witness box. "That were a leading question, Mr Lane," interjected the chairman. "Yes, sir," said Lane, "but this is cross-examination." "Now then, young man," was the reply, "don't make excuses."

Mr Ralph Cleworth, Stipendiary Magistrate for the City of Leeds, returned home one evening, after a day in court, to see his wife kneeling in front of the fireplace, sweeping up some ashes. She was wearing a dress which he recognised, and he tapped her affectionately on the bottom. The housemaid got up, greatly embarrassed. She had been given the dress by Mrs Cleworth that very morning!

A solicitor, usually instructed in the magistrates' court for the defence, one day appeared for the prosecution. "Good morning Mr Smith," said the chairman, "how nice to see you on our side for a change!"

A lady appeared before the Leeds magistrates' court charged with keeping a disorderly house. Defence counsel secured her acquittal. She expressed her gratitude to him in no uncertain terms: "Any time you have half an hour to spare come along and see me. I've got some beautiful girls. You will enjoy yourself. That's the least I can do to thank you." That evening counsel told his wife what had happened, and what his client had said. His wife's reply was,

"Love, if you want to go, you go! It's time you disappointed someone else!"

A different lady in the witness box of the same magistrates' court on a similar charge was defended by a highly respectable solicitor. She was describing the layout of her premises, getting very muddled, and making a mess of it. In the end, exasperated, she said to her solicitor, "Go on, Joe, you tell them. You've been there often enough."

Court clerk to defendant: "Is your name Winston Jones?" No reply, so the clerk repeats his question. Still no reply, so the judge tries, "What is your name, sir?" To this the defendant replies, "You mean you took all dis time and you brought me all dis way, and you don't even know my name?"

The magistrates' clerk at a Yorkshire magistrates' court was always anxious for a short day, and the following scenario was not uncommon:
Clerk to defendant: "To this charge how do you plead?"
Defendant: "Not guilty."
Clerk (in voice of utter disbelief): "Not what?"
Defendant: "Guilty, sir."
Clerk: "That's better." (To the Bench): "The defendant pleads guilty, sir."

A witness was asked by the clerk of the court: "Are you content to be sworn on the New Testament? Or do you wish to have the Old Testament?" The witness replied, "Why? Is there a difference."

A case was being heard by the local magistrates' court. The chairman of the Bench was the local baker. After a contested hearing the Bench found the case proved, and announced this in court. The chairman then said to the defendant, "Have you anything to say?" He replied, "Yes. Cancel my bread order."

Probation officer to magistrates: "It will be a great risk if this man is placed on probation."
Defendant, gripping the dock rails: "I'll take the risk, sir."

Probation-speak is something to which all barristers have to get accustomed, and frequently to translate. A recent probation report said of a client, "He cannot relate to the dynamics of his siblings. His nuclear family is multi-delinquent with a high incarceration index."

A magistrate, with a slip of the tongue, said to the defendant in passing sentence: "I sentence you to nine months in a Youth Hostel."

A motorist, having unfortunately taken too much drink, had a slight accident. He was not hurt, and made his way to a nearby telephone box and rang the police. "I have done a naughty thing," he said, "a naughty, naughty thing ... I want to tell you that I've just knocked over some of those pretty little bollards and a workman's hut." "Excuse me, sir," said the police officer at the other end of the line, "Where are you speaking from." "Ah," said the motorist, "Wouldn't you like to know!"

Police officers do not invariably make the correct deduction, or perhaps sometimes they do not hear the Bench very clearly. The following is a case in point:
Magistrate to police officer: "What is the charge against this defendant?"
Police officer: "She is charged with uttering a forged bank-note for the purpose of gain."
Magistrate? "Ah, counterfeit."
Police officer: "Yes. She had two."

Police officer to suspect: "I want you to accompany me to the police station."
Suspect: "Why?"
Police Officer: "Because I'm terrified of going alone."

In the witness box was a merchant seaman who was asked the question: "What did you say at the time?" He seemed reluctant to answer, showing some embarrassment, but at last he said, "B----r me through my oilskins." The chairman of the Bench with great presence of mind said, "I think the witness means he was taken aback!"

Late at night in the City of London a policeman happens to see a man hanging round a lamp post in Moorgate. When he approaches, the man says, "Where does the Lord Mayor live?" The policeman looks at him hard and then says, "My lord, you *are* the Lord Mayor."

Chairman of a magistrates' court (who happened to be a funeral director) to defendant: "We order you to be cremated to the Crown Court."

Barrister in Leeds magistrates' court (to small boy who alleged he was the witness of a motor accident): "I suggest to you that at the time of the incident in question you and your friend, walking home from school, had passed the road junction where the collision occurred."
Small boy: "You're right, sir, we had, we was a long way past."
Barrister: "It follows therefore that you could not have seen the collision."
Small boy: "You're wrong, sir. I saw it clear as day. I were walking backwards."

ROUND THE BRITISH ISLES

This story goes back to the days when farm servants were paid (at least in Yorkshire) just once a year. When Martinmas came round, one lad told his master: "Ah's thinking o' gannin' doon inti Driffield tineet. Can Ah sub fahve shillin' o' my wages?" "Nay, Ah can't hear what thoo says," said the old man. "Thoo better come roond ti t'other lug." Feeling that the atmosphere was not too hostile, the lad decided to try for a bigger sum, and bawled: "Ah's wanting ti gan doon inti Driffield tineet. Can Ah sub ten shillin' o' my wages?" "Nay," said the master, "Ah can't hear a word thoo says. Thoo'd better gan back ti t'fahve shillin' lug."

Lord Asquith once said of Yorkshire: "It is a beautiful county. I remember it for the serene beauty of its cathedrals, the majestic eloquence of its advocates and the truly remarkable carnality of its inhabitants."

A Yorkshireman is the butt of many jokes, generally directed at the thriftiness which is a county characteristic. A Yorkshireman has long pockets and short hands, they say; he never walks up an escalator, always stands still in order to get his money's worth, and would rather spill blood than beer. But perhaps best of all is the saying that a Yorkshireman is a Scotsman stripped of his generosity.

The Queen was attending a reception at the Lord Mayor's House in York and was speaking to a rather nervous Yorkshire lady who said to her, "Do I call you 'Ma'am' or 'Your Majesty'?" The Queen replied, "I don't think it matters; you've already called me "love" three times."

A Conservative politician once said to Harold Wilson, "They say you were born in Yorkshire." "Not only born there, but forged there as well," replied Wilson. The Conservative replied: "I always thought you were counterfeit."

Never ask a man if he's a Yorkshireman. If he is, within five minutes he will tell you so. If he isn't, you will only humiliate him.

What is the difference between a Yorkshireman and his photograph? The photograph is fully developed.

A lady in Halifax was told that a young man had discovered a fire in his house and had come down a drainpipe to escape from it. To this she replied, "He must have been right thin."

You can always tell a Yorkshireman but you can't tell him much.

A visitor from Texas was visiting a Yorkshire farmer and asked him how big his farm was. The Yorkshireman replied, "From that tree to this tree and o'er there to the homestead." "Gee," said the Texan, "I got a farm, and if I leave home in the morning at 6 am to go round my farm I don't get back home till 6 pm." "I know what you mean," said the Yorkshire farmer, "you're right unlucky - my dad had a car like that."

"How's business?" said one Bradford business man to another. "Business is that bad that even them as don't intend to pay 'ave stopped ordering," was the reply.

At a time of economic boom a Keighley accountant's reply to the same question was rather different, but as far as he was concerned, along the same lines. "There's a slump in liquidations!", he said.

A farmer's wife asked her husband to tell their teenage son the facts of life. He responded thus: "Does t'a remember lad, coming back from t'market t'other day, we seen a young man and a young woman in t'hayfield?" "Aye, dad," said the lad. "Well does t'a remember what they was up to?" "Aye, dad." "Well, t'birds and t'bees do t'same as them."

A motorist was completely lost in the fastnesses of the Yorkshire Dales. He stopped the car and walked to the nearest farmstead to ask for directions and happened to ask the farmer why there were no signposts. To this the farmer replied, "Them as lives here knows. Them as doesn't know doesn't come."

The same insularity was manifested by a Sedbergh grocer who was asked by a visitor for a jar of decaffeinated coffee. The shopkeeper's reply was, "You're the third person who's asked for that today, and I keep telling you there's no demand for it."

A Yorkshireman was enthusing to a friend about the beauty of his wrist watch. "This is a beautiful watch," he said, "I shall always treasure it because on his deathbed my dear grandfather sold it to me."

A West Riding businessman said to a friend whom he met in a Bradford street, "I hear tell that tha's had a fire at thee mill." "Sh! Sh!" the friend replied, "It's not till next week."

Judges do not always find it easy to follow the local vernacular. This seems to have been the case in a trial at Leeds Assizes before Mr Justice Slade. A female witness said, "It worra reet cold neet, and I telled me son to mend t'fire." The judge said, "Mend the fire? Why, madam, was the fire broken?"

A Yorkshire farmer named Foster many years ago used to go to the local public house every Saturday night and imbibe a considerable quantity of beer. His practice was to park his horse and cart unattended outside the public house and when he left at a late hour, the worse for wear, to climb into the driver's seat, say "Gee up," to the horse and go off to sleep. Away the horse would go, knowing exactly the road home. One day his friends thought they would play a trick on him, so after he had gone into the pub, they loosened the horse and off it went home leaving the cart behind. When the farmer came out, he climbed into his usual seat on the car and promptly went to sleep. He woke up in the middle of the night, looked around and said, "If my name's Foster, I've lost an 'oss. If my name isn't Foster, I've fun a cart."

A dutiful Yorkshire nephew said to his down-to-earth Yorkshire uncle, "I am going to buy you a book for your birthday," to which the uncle replied, "Don't bother. I've already got one."

A Yorkshireman was invited to a very upmarket official dinner at the Savoy Hotel in London. Soon after the guests sat down, a waiter moved round with a plate of gull's eggs. When proffered the plate, the Yorkshireman took six on to his own plate. "Hey lad," he said to the waiter, "what do I do with these?" The waiter replied haughtily, "Sir, you put four of them back."

A sorrowing Yorkshire husband was arranging for a headstone for his deceased wife's grave, and gave an order to the stonemason that the inscription should read, "Lord, she was thine." When the headstone was done, he had a look at it in the mason's yard, and saw that the inscription read, "Lord she was thin." He told the mason that he had left an "e" out, and asked for it to be put right. Next week he returned and found that the inscription now read, "E, Lord she was thin."

The husband of a rather garrulous Yorkshire woman died. A few days later her friend asked her what were her husband's last words. "Last words!" she said, "Last words! He didn't have any last words. I was with him to the end."

A defendant was charged in a Yorkshire Crown Court with stealing sheep. The case was not strong, and defence counsel made the most of it and the jury in due course, acquitted the defendant. Counsel was curious to know which of his points had attracted the jury most, and casually asked one of the jurors after the case why they had acquitted. "Well," he said, "It were like this. T'chap who stole t'sheep were on t'jury."

R.M. Clough of counsel, defending a shepherd at Leeds Assizes on a sheep stealing charge asked the shepherd, "What is the relative incidence of twins in sheep and humans?" The shepherd replied, "I'll tell thee what, lad, if thou'll leave t'ewes to me, I'll leave t'women to thee."

An Australian visitor to England was walking in the Yorkshire Dales. Looking over a wall at the head of Swaledale he happened to see a farmer struggling in the field with a sheep. "Good day, cobber," said the Ozzie, "Shearing?" No, I'm not," was the reply, "You find your own bloody sheep."

"If you put a bull in a field," said the man in the pub at Buckden, "you don't expect to see a lot of calves frisking about the next morning." "No," said the farmer standing next to him, "but you'd see a lot of happy faces."

The senior boys of a famous Yorkshire school were dining in an upstairs room at the Royal Station Hotel in York. One or two had too much to drink and instead of taking the main staircase towards the exit, they took a staircase which led directly to the railway tracks, and began walking along the lines towards Thirsk. After a while one said to the other, "I say, that was a good dinner, but there are a lot of steps in this hotel." "I wouldn't mind that," his companion replied, "but the bloody bannisters are so low."

A village lad from Upper Wharfedale was attending an interview at Leeds University for a place in the law school. He was asked what was the meaning of the phrase "audi alteram partem." His reply was, "Parts for German cars are hard to get."

Fred, who lived in Keighley and had a business in Bradford, was well-known to be slightly mean. He was interested in joining the Freemasons, and asked his friend what would be the advantages of membership. His friend, as a leg-pull, said that free railway travel was one of the benefits, provided that one made the secret sign. Fred asked what the secret sign was, and was told that he must ask the booking clerk three times for his ticket, and each time circle the palm of his hand clockwise in front of his face. Next day Fred thought he would try this out, so went to the booking office at Keighley station and said to the clerk, "Ticket for Bradford," three times with the accompanying secret sign. The booking clerk, who had been put in the picture and been given the money for the ticket by the friend, handed the ticket over without question. Unfortunately that evening after work when Fred asked the booking clerk at Bradford for a ticket to Keighley, the clerk asked for the money. "But I'm a mason," said Fred. "I don't care if you're the King of England," said the clerk, "the ticket costs two pounds ten." So Fred, very cross, had to pay, and when he got back to Keighley, the first person he saw on leaving the station was his friend. He complained that he had had to pay for his ticket at Bradford, and his friend asked him whether he had given the secret sign. Fred said he had, and did a demonstration. "Oh," said the friend, "that's where you went wrong. You were coming back! You should have circled your hand the other way."

An actor visiting Sheffield was looking for inexpensive digs. He found a place which looked suitable, and the landlady invited him in and showed him to a bedroom on the fifth floor. There was of course no lift. She apologised for the fact that the only lavatory was five floors down, but she explained that she had provided a chamber pot which was beneath the bed. "But think on," she said, "if you have to use t'potty in t'night, don't put it back under t'bed. T'steam rots t'springs!"

"Since you'll have to wear breeches at banquets," the duchess told a young Yorkshireman who was applying for a footman's job, "please roll up your trousers and let me look at your calves." When he had done so, she added with a nod, "and as you'll be wearing a kilt when we're in Scotland, roll them up further and show me your knees." He obliged, and she nodded again. "Fine," she said, "all that remains is for me to see your testimonials." That evening in the pub the prospective footman said to his friend, "If only I'd 'ad a better education I'd 've got that job."

Late one night a man answered the phone, picked it up and after listening to the caller said, "How do I know? Ask the Met Office." "Who was that, darling?" said his wife. "It was some stupid man wanting to know if the coast was clear," he replied.

A family in Yorkshire happened to employ a live-in domestic help who was not too bright. On one occasion the family were expecting a call from Canada but the help answered the telephone, listened for a moment and then said, "Of course it is." Her employer asked who rang to which her reply was, "It was some silly man on the line saying, 'It's a long distance from Toronto'."

A hostel for ex-prisoners was built in a rather high-class area of a Northern city. Soon after its completion and occupation a lady who lived nearby approached the warden and said, "Do I understand that there are ex-prisoners living here?" "Yes," said the warden. "Good," she said, "I thought they were students."

Welsh juries are against crime, but they're not dogmatic about it.

There are two things between the Welsh and the English - trust and understanding. We don't trust you. You don't understand us.

After a heavy night out in Swansea after the rugby, a couple of Welshmen decided to take a bus from the bus garage to get themselves home up the valleys. One stood guard at the garage door, while the other went in to get hold of a bus. Instead of a minute or two, it took him half-an-hour. When he emerged at the wheel of the double-decker, his friend asked him where he had been all that time. "Oh," he said, "the Pontardulais bus was at the back."

A Cardiff bus driver was caught by an inspector in the evening of an international match day at the Arms Park, taking a single-decker from the bus garage to give a lift home to a member of the Welsh team. "Hang on a minute bach," said the inspector, "you should take a double decker. He may want to smoke."

Wales were playing England at the Arms Park, and little Tommy was in his seat in the North Stand. "Hello Tommy, said the man in the next seat, "where's your dad?" "He's at home looking for the ticket," the young man replied.

During the Second War a German spy was briefed to contact a Welsh agent living at an address, 5 Railway Terrace, Tremsarron. Unknown to the Germans, the agent had moved. The spy landed near Haverfordwest and made his way to 5 Railway Terrace. He knocked at the door and said to the man who came to the door, the codewords, "The snows are melting over Snowdonia." "It's not me you want," said the occupant, "It's Jones the spy; he lives across the road."

It is always said that the people of West Wales are very careful about money. This is illustrated by the experience of a well-known cricketer who was visiting his friend who lived in a cottage along the Pembrokeshire coast. He found his friend and his wife scraping the wallpaper off the walls. "Decorating?" he asked. "No. Moving" was the reply.

Those in charge of the Welsh Eisteddfod decided that, in order to give it a face-lift, they would introduce a dirty limerick competition. Entries were invited, and in due course the winner was announced, but the limerick was not published. A newspaper sent a reporter up to Bangor to ask to see it, and was told that it was copyright and he would have to see the authors, the Misses Jones who lived at 2 Rose Cottages, Machynlleth. He went to Rose Cottages, knocked on the door, and asked to see the winning limerick. Blodwyn said, "It's copyright, boyo, but I'll go and see what my sister Angharad says about it." Off she went and quickly came back. "My sister says you can't have the poem, but I'll read it to you. To save embarrassment, when I get to a rude word I'll just say dum-dee. Is that OK?" The reporter agreed, so Blodwyn said, "It goes like this:
Dum-dee Dum-dee Dum-dee
Dum-dee Dum-dee Dum-dee
Dum-dee
Dum-dee
Dum-dee Dum-dee F-----g bastard."

When I read the local paper I knew at once that I was in Wales. The report read: "At the funeral Myfanwy Evans broke her ankle against the gravestone, which cast gloom over the whole proceedings."

A firm in the executive jet plane taxi business had arranged a demonstration afternoon near Cardigan and was selling pleasure flights. Business was slack, so one pilot said to a local who seemed to be very interested that he would take him and his wife up for a few minutes for free if neither of them said a word. This was agreed, so up they went, and when they came down the Welshman said to the pilot, "It was very nice, but when the window broke and I saw my wife going out, I nearly shouted!"

If one is ever asked why it is that Welshmen always go round in threes the answer is: "One to read, one to write, and one to keep the two intellectuals out of trouble."

A Welsh prop forward hasn't got a neck. His head is connected directly to his spine. And a Welshman's idea of hell is somewhere where you have to put the ball into the scrum straight.

Boss to business executive: "I hired you on intuition, I gave you a rise on intuition, I promoted you on intuition, I am firing you after a great deal of thought."

In the words of a Welsh miner: "In a collision there you are. In an explosion where are you?"

Judge Hill-Kelly, whom many members of the Bar thought to be pedantic and slightly ill-tempered, was hearing a possession case in the Cardiff County Court. The case turned on the right of a female defendant under the terms of her lease to remain in the premises. She, in the witness box, claimed that she was. "But madam," said the judge, "Madam, look at the Habendum." "I can't, your Honour," she replied, "I'm a married woman!" One wonders what she thought he meant!

The most westerly public house in the Gower peninsula is surrounded by rocks on the landward side of the Worms Head, near Rhossili. An English visitor went into the pub on a hot summer afternoon and asked the barman for a large whisky on the rocks. The barman said, "There'll be an extra charge, boyo, if you drink it outside."

A young unmarried lady from North Wales found herself to be pregnant. She felt that she ought to consult a doctor, but did not want the matter to become the subject of local gossip, so decided to go up to London to consult a doctor who had been recommended to her by a girl friend as being of good Welsh descent and good for that sort of thing. His name was Dr Vaughan Williams. When she arrived at Paddington and asked at the information desk for the doctor's address, the clerk on duty told her that the Albert Hall was the place. Arriving at the Albert Hall she asked the commissionaire if she could see Dr Vaughan Williams. "No," said the official, "He's far too busy. At the moment he's orchestrating the Men of Harlech," to which the lady replied, "Eight months too late!"

"My pal Dai Morgan had a bad night, see, and next morning I counted he was ten seconds late getting fell in on parade. The sergeant-major sees him (he has eyes like a hawk has our sergeant-major) and goes right up to him, looks him in the eyes and says, "You 'orrible Welshman, you are late on parade!" Back comes Dai Morgan, quick as a flash, and witty too, "F--k you," says he."

A Scotsman won a newspaper competition, the prize for which was a weekend trip to London to see the sights. He had never been to London before, and when he got back to Wester Ross his friends asked him how he liked it and how he got on. "I've only one complaint," he said, "I was staying in this hotel and all the time there was knocking. First they knocked on my door, then they knocked on the floor, and finally they knocked on the ceiling." "And what did you do?" his friends asked. "Och I didn'a take nae notice. I just carried on playing my bagpipes!"

A client telephoned to an Edinburgh firm of solicitors. The person answering said, "This is Macpherson, Macpherson and Macpherson. How can I help you?" The client said, "May I speak to Mr Macpherson please?" "Och no," was the reply, "he's at a meeting." "Well, may I speak to Mr Macpherson then?" "No, he's seeing a client." "Well may I speak to Mr Macpherson?" "Aye" was the reply, "Speaking!"

The Scots keep the Sabbath and anything else they can get their hands on. Before they cast their bread on the waters they make sure the tide is coming in.

A Scotsman once said, "They tell me it takes a surgical operation to get a joke into a Scotsman's head, but I don't see how you could get a joke into anyone's head by a surgical operation."

Lord Tweedsmuir once asked a friend what in his opinion was the finest view in the world. His friend replied, "Why, The Cloch Light from Gourock of course!" In an effort to try and persuade him to broaden his horizons, the next question was what he considered to be the second-best view in the world. To this the reply was, "Gourock from the Cloch Light."

A Scotsman was shipwrecked on a desert island, and lived alone for three years, scraping an existence like Robinson Crusoe from plants and nuts. After three years, a very pretty female stepped ashore and said to the Scot, "You may have three wishes and they will be granted." The first wish he made was obviously for a wee dram. The second was for a dish of haggis. Both were granted. "For your third wish," said the lady, "would you not like to play around with me?" "Aye," said the Scot, "This is too much. What a bonny lass! First whisky, then haggis. Now she is offering me a game of golf."

In the course of the royal visit to South Africa, a local Afrikaans speaker said to the Queen Mother, "I can't be very enthusiastic about your visit because in the past we have had a lot of trouble with the English." She replied, "I know exactly what you mean. In Scotland we feel precisely the same!"

On a visit made by Sir James Clark to London from Edinburgh, a Southerner was mocking his Scots accent by saying to him, "I didn't know that water was spelt with two 't's." Quick as a flash, Sir James replied, "Water is nae spelt with two t's, but manners is spelt with two n's."

An Englishman had a theory that no Irishman could answer a question by saying Yes or No. He travelled the length and breadth of Ireland without success, but he thought that at least in Dublin he might succeed. He found himself outside the Post Office in O'Connell Street. "Is this the Post Office?" he asked a woman who was passing by. "Is it stamps you be wanting?" she replied.

An Irish priest was feeling very depressed and consulted his doctor who advised him to take off his dog collar and see how the other half lived. So he did just that, and went off to London where he ended up at the Playboy Club. There he was served by a rather gorgeous bunny girl who said, as she served him, "Father O'Flaherty, you're a long way from home." "Goodness gracious, Sister Theresa, what are you doing here?" he asked, surprised. "Well, father," she said, " it must be that we both have the same doctor."

A husband arrived home one evening to find his wife in bed with another man. Without more ado he produced a hand-gun and shot his wife's friend. He then held the revolver to his own head, at which his wife started laughing uncontrollably. "Don't laugh so hard," said the husband, "You're next."

A visitor from Spain was travelling on a train from Dublin to Belfast. In the course of the journey he asked the gentleman sitting opposite, "Do you have in your language the equivalent of the Spanish word 'mañana'?" "Begorra we do," was the reply, "but in our language it does not have the same exquisite sense of urgency."

To an Irishman a yellow line means no parking at all, and a double yellow line means no parking at all at all.

In the agony aunt section of *The Dublin Courier* appeared the question, "What are the requirements of a valid marriage?" The reply given was this: "The requirements are threefold: erectio, penetratio and emissio. If any one of these three is missing the marriage is invalid, as it is also if they are in the wrong order."

The man knocked at the door and asked a lady of the house if she had any odd jobs she would like him to do. She said, "Yes. Go round the back of the house and paint the porch. Here's some green paint and a brush." Two hours later the man went back to the door and said to the lady "All done, mum, but it wasn't a Porsche it was a Mercedes!"

If you ask an Irishman what he thinks of the Renault 5, he will say they ought to be released at once.

An Irishman was asked how many seconds there are in a year. "Twelve," he replied, "2nd of January, 2nd of February ...."

The whole world seems to descend on Dublin when England are playing Ireland at rugby at Lansdowne Road. Walking through the centre of the city an Englishman met an Irish friend who lived in London. "Hi! Paddy," he said, "How did you come over, by plane or by ferry?" "I don't know," his friend replied, "my wife got the tickets."

Have you heard of the Irishman in a public house saying to his next door neighbour at the bar, "I shouldn't be here. I should be at home with my wife and children." "Why aren't you?" he was asked. "Because I don't have any," he replied.

He was up for trial on a murder charge. The evidence was very strong, but the defendant's brother happened to be on the jury, and received firm instructions from the family to make sure that the jury brought in a verdict of manslaughter. The jury convicted of manslaughter and the family were delighted, and asked the brother later how he did it. "I brought them round," he said, "they wanted to find him not guilty."

There are many stories about space travel in its early days when animals of various types were sent into spare. This one concerns a space capsule sent up with an Irishman in charge and a monkey on board. Both were given sealed instructions to be opened on orders from Mission Control. The monkey's instructions read, "Press digits 2 19 37 54 and 108 on the handset, adjust computer, take azimuth bearing eastern edge of sun and report on cloud cover earth." The Irishman's were, "Feed the bloody monkey."

Three labourers on a building site were asked at the end of the week by the foreman to sign for their wages. Paddy signed by putting one cross and saying, "That's my name." Murphy put two crosses saying, "That's my Christian name and my surname." Seamus put three crosses saying, "That's my Christian name. My surname and my degree at Dublin University."

An Irishman in London applies for a job on a building site. The foreman does not think very highly of the Irish, so asks him the difficult question, "Do you know the difference between joist and girder?" "Yes," was the reply, "Joyce wrote Ulysses and Goethe wrote Faust."

A suspect was standing on an identity parade in respect of a charge of rape. The victim was led into the parade by the duty police sergeant. As soon as she entered the room the suspect shouted, "That's her!"

A labourer on a building site was working at a tremendous rate. Every two minutes he dashed up a ladder with an enormous load of bricks. After this had been going on for an hour, a friend asked him why he was working so hard. "Oh," he said, "don't tell anyone, but I've got them all fooled. I'm not really working hard at all - it's the same load of bricks every time."

A man in a pub asked another, "Was it you or your brother who died in Leeds?" The other replied, "It must have been my brother. I was never in Leeds in the whole of me life."

An English visitor to Dublin took a taxi from the airport to the Gresham Hotel. On the way the taxi-driver went through all the traffic lights at red. When asked why, he said, "Well, I was taught to drive by me brother Danny, and me brother Danny always does that." Eventually he stopped at a green light. When asked why, he replied, "Well, me brother Danny might be coming the other way."

The same English visitor asked the hall porter for a morning paper. "Do you want yesterday's or today's," was the porter's reply. "Why, today's, of course," said the Englishman! "Well, you'll have to wait till tomorrow for that," was the reply.

Irish toast: May you be in Heaven half an hour before the devil knows you're dead.

There was a sad occasion in Dublin when a man employed at the brewery drowned in a vat of Guinness. A friend at once went round to see the deceased's wife to tell her the news. "I hope he didn't suffer much," she said. "No," said the friend, "he crawled out three times to go to the toilet."

"Can you help me out?"
"Certainly, which way did you come in?"

MEN FROM THE MINISTRY

A member of the House of Lords was dining at his London club, and had asked three times for a glass of water, without result. In the end, he called the young waiter over and said, "I have asked several times for a glass of water. Do you know who I am?" "No," replied the waiter, "but if your lordship gives me a few moments, I'll soon find out for you."

A Member of Parliament who habitually kept late hours returned home one evening to find that his wife had left him a note saying: "The day before yesterday you came home yesterday. Yesterday you came home today. If today you come home tomorrow you will find that I left you yesterday."

A politician's analysis of the English press runs as follows:
The Times is read by the people who run the country;
The Mirror is read by the people who think they run the country;
The Guardian is read by the people who think they ought to run the country;
The Independent is read by the people who think the country ought to be run by another country;
The Financial Times is read by the people who own the country;
The Daily Mail is read by the people who think the country ought to be run as it used to be;
The Daily Telegraph is read by the people who still think it is;
The Sun is read by the people who don't care who runs the country so long as she has a large bust.

George Washington couldn't tell a lie; Lloyd George couldn't tell the truth; Harold Wilson couldn't tell the difference.

It was a pet theory of one of the Presidents of the United States that people never listen to things which are said to them on social occasions, and to prove it he decided, when standing to receive a line of guests at a party in the White House, to slip in, while uttering words of welcome, the phrase, "I just shot my mother-in-law." At least a hundred guests heard this without showing any sign that it had registered. But the next guest heard it, paused, and then said, "Well, Mr President, I guess she sure had it coming to her."

A young American couple were discussing the well-known reluctance of President Calvin Coolidge to speak. The husband bet the wife that if she could engage the President in a conversation which resulted in him saying not less than three words, he would give her fifty dollars. The matter was put to the test a few weeks later when the wife attended a White House reception. She approached the President and explained that she stood to win fifty dollars if he would adorn the occasion by speaking three words or more. To this his reply was short and succinct. "You lose," he said.

A new entrant to the Diplomatic Service was invited to a reception at a South American embassy in Mayfair. In due course music began, and he took the floor with a very pretty girl who happened to be standing next to him at the time. After a short time, the couple were interrupted by an embassy official who said, "This is wrong!" "Why?" said the young diplomat, "What's wrong with having a waltz with a pretty girl?" "What's wrong sir," said the official, "is first, that this isn't a waltz, it's the Uruguayan national anthem, and second, this isn't a pretty girl, it's the Cardinal Archbishop of Montevideo."

A civil servant one morning found a file in his in-tray. He initialled it and sent it on. Next day it appeared on his desk again with the comment: "This file had nothing to do with you and you had no business to initial it. Kindly erase your initials and initial the erasure!"

Higher civil servants are reputed to have four trays ; In, Out, Pending and LTU (Laugh and Tear Up).

John Major was once heard to say "I have been doing a little family research recently. I've managed to trace my family back as far as my father. Which is more than many of my colleagues could!"

In the course of a visit to Moscow Mr Major was granted an audience with Boris Yeltsin. In the course of the conversation he said to Mr Yeltsin, "Boris, what in a word, is the condition of Russia today?" Yeltsin replied, "Good." "Yes," said Mr Major, but how would you put it in two words?" "Not good," was the reply!

The Queen was present at Victoria Station awaiting the arrival of an African Head of State. When he arrived he was shown to an open landau which he shared with the Queen on the return journey to Buckingham Palace. As they went along, the carriage horses persistently passed wind. The Queen held her tongue for a long time, but at last she said, "Sorry about that," to which her guest replied, "Oh, if your Majesty had not mentioned it, I would have thought it was the horses!"

The Duke of Devonshire, many years ago, dreamed that he was addressing the House of Lords, woke up and found that he was.

My friend is a great orator. Before he speaks he doesn't know what he's going to say. While he's speaking he hardly knows what he's saying, and when he sits down he can't remember what he's said.

The Earl of Sandwich was back in the House of Lords after an illness, and was greeted there by a political opponent who said, "So ... you're back! Never mind, you'll soon be dead, either in the noose or with the pox." To this the noble Earl replied, "That, sir, depends on whether I embrace your morals or your mistress."

The difference between the political parties is said to be the following:
Conservatism: You have two cows.
Socialism: You have two cows; the government takes both and gives you the milk.
Communism: You have two cows; the government takes both and sells you the milk.
Fascism: You have two cows; the government takes both and shoots you.
Capitalism: You have two cows: you sell one and buy a bull.

Two stories are told of Viscount Castleross, who had a large midriff and a ready wit. A lady at a party said to him, "What have you got in there?" To this he replied, "An elephant ma'am! Would you like to see its trunk?" At a different party another lady said to him, "If that was on a woman I'd know what it was!" to which he replied, "Madam, it was last night. What was it?"

An MP was attending a garden party in his constituency. A rather plain lady was trying to approach him but was headed off by his secretary and his team. A few days later he received a letter which read, "Dear Mr Smith, I tried to speak to you the other day at the garden party, but I didn't manage to. I so admire you and your work, and I wonder if you would give me your autograph. Yours sincerely, Margaret Jones (horseface)." Rather touched by her modesty, the MP sent off to her a distinguished photograph of himself and inscribed it: "To Horseface, with my very best wishes." The following day his secretary asked him whether he had replied to the letter from the plain-looking lady at the garden party and said, "I put 'horseface' after her name so that you would know who she was."

AT COLLEGE

When a lady enters a room, the Wykehamist calls out for somebody to fetch a chair, the Etonian goes and gets one, the Harrovian sits down in the chair himself.

The Dean of a Cambridge college asked a freshman for his name and was told it was Chung Hoo. When asked if that had a meaning the young man replied that it meant Son of God. "Don't let that embarrass you," said the Dean, "in this college we have the sons of some other very distinguished men."

An impromptu debate was arranged by the law faculty at Edinburgh University. Speakers were given a piece of paper on which was written the topic on which they were to speak for not less than two minutes. The paper handed to a Scots judge read, "Whisky and water." The judge thought for a minute and then said, "Speaking as a Scot, you never mix the two. Speaking as a judge it is a felony to make the first in private and a misdemeanour to make the second in public!"

On an occasion many years ago a group of people were standing on Cambridge station. One was the philosopher Ludwig Wittgenstein and with him were two friends, all of them talking learnedly about philosophy. The train came in, and as it went out, the two friends caught it, leaving the Professor behind, standing on the platform. An old lady came up and commiserated with him on having missed the train, to which he replied, "Madam, I have a problem, but my friends have an even bigger problem. They came here to see me off."

Four students in the Department of Physics at Berkeley University decided to have a night out before their termly examination. They dined and drank so well that they slept in, and arrived on campus too late to sit the exam. They went to see the professor and cooked

145

up the explanation that the reason for their late arrival was that the car in which they had been travelling to the University had blown a tyre, and as they had no spare wheel on board, they were stuck. The professor appeared to be very sympathetic and told them that he would, as a great indulgence, allow them to sit the examination the next day. Next day their papers contained two questions. The first (for which it said 5 per cent of the total marks would be awarded) was a complicated one on astro-physics. The second (attracting 95 per cent of the marks) was simple. It read: "Which tyre?"

The wife of the Warden of All Souls' College Oxford is reputed to have said to a visiting dignitary, "My husband says that you can learn all about science in a fortnight." The dignitary, blessed with an acid wit, replied, "What a pity your husband never had a fortnight to spare."

At the end of a lecture, the Professor of Logic was asked a question by a student at the back of the lecture room. To this he gave the following reply: "I know you believe you understand what you think I said, but I am not sure you realise that what you heard is not what I meant!"

"Despite a most tremendous thirst,
He none the less achieved a first."

AT CHURCH

It was once said of a bishop, one hopes not with any truth, that "such time as was not spent on personal adornment was devoted to neglect of his duty."

A not very erudite parishioner was telling a clergyman that he ought to write a book of his experiences and his sermons. "Well, perhaps one day," the clergyman replied, "and I might publish it posthumously." "Well, don't leave it too long," came the reply.

A parson attended a London drinks party and, unfortunately took a little too much drink on board. As he was walking home, he happened to pass a flat on the door of which was a brass plate which said "PAUL."The parson rang the bell, and after some delay a man answered the door. The parson said to him, "I congratulate you on that marvellous letter to the Ephesians." "Oh, go home! You're drunk," said the man. A few yards down the road, the parson stopped, turned round, returned and rang the bell again. When the occupant came to the door he said, "That letter to the Ephesians. Did you ever get a reply?"

One day a parson in the course of his sermon asked any member of the congregation who was absolutely pure and without sin to stand up and be counted. A man at the back of the church stood up. "Are you absolutely pure and without sin?" the parson asked him. "No, I'm not," the man replied, "but I'm standing in for my wife's first husband."

The parson delivered a moving sermon on the beauties of the after-life and then asked his congregation to put up their hands all those who wanted to go to heaven. All did so, except one old man. "Don't you want to go there, Silas?", asked the surprised cleric. "Not if this lot's going too!" came the reply.

Some years ago in West Wales the local preacher was in full flood. "I'm going to tell you today," he said to his congregation, "about the flames of Hell. If you were to pour the waters of the River Towey into the jaws of Hell, it would be as nothing. If you were to pour the waters of the River Towey and the waters of the River Teifi into the jaws of Hell it would be as nothing. If you were to pour into the jaws of Hell the waters of the River Towey and the waters of the River Teifi and all the waters of the seven oceans of the world, it would be no more than a *"Psst"* to a red-hot-flat-iron!"

In the same chapel on a different occasion the preacher was telling the congregation of the omnipresence of the devil. "The devil is everywhere," he said, "He is here in the front row with the widow Thomas, he is there in the middle of the chapel with Dai Morgan, he is on the back row with Griffith Jones, and he is up in the balcony with Huw Davis." There was a long pause as the message sank in. Then a voice from the balcony rang out, "Hey, preacher. B----r's loose!"

There was a banging on the door of the Manse late one night and the Minister went down to see what was the matter. A voice outside the door said, "I'm gaye troubled aboot the schisms in the church." "That's as may be," said the Minister, "but it's very late and you must go home. You're very drunk." "That's as may be," said the voice, "but ma troubles must be put at rest the noo." "No," said the Minister, "come and see me when you're sober in the morning." "When I'm sober in the morning," said the voice, "I dinna give a f--k aboot the schisms in the church."

Barristers and parsons both invite constructive criticism of their performance. One parson visiting a Yorkshire parish in order to take a service and give a sermon asked the rector for how long he ought to speak. "Far be it from me to abridge the message of the gospel," his friend replied, "but we have no recorded case in this parish of any sinner being saved after 10 minutes." The verger was also asked for his advice, and he said, "Well, sir, the only advice I've got to give is this: Speak up! The agnostics in this building are something terrible."

The vicar always knew from the way a letter from his bishop began whether it contained good news or bad. If the former it began, "I have decided ..." If the latter it began, "After a night of anxious prayer ..."

The Archbishop of Canterbury, when asked why he was so sunburnt, replied, "My kitchen sink faces South."

A parishioner gave her priest a bottle of cherry brandy. The priest sent her a little note which read: "Thank you for the fruit and the spirit in which it was given."

When giving character evidence, parsons are notoriously unpredictable. This was demonstrated in an embezzlement case at Bolton Quarter Sessions, when defence counsel called the rector of the defendant's church as a character witness. "Do you know this man?" was the first question. "Yes," was the answer. "Is he a pillar of your church and does he help with the tuning of the church organ?" "Yes." "And, tell the court, would you be happy to entrust him with money?" There was then a long and anxious pause, at the end of which the parson leaned forward and said in a hoarse voice, "How much?"

The President of the USA was visiting the Pope. In His Holiness's study was a telephone coloured red. During the visit the Pope picked up the phone and asked to speak to the Chief Rabbi in Jerusalem. At the end of the call he checked the charge which was, he was told, 10 dollars. He then picked up the phone and asked for the Boss. The President asked him the cost of that call, to which the Pope replied 10 cents. "What's the difference?" asked the President. "Well, from here," replied the Pope, "it's a local call."

A bishop was invited by the rector to preach on a Sunday evening at a village church. When he arrived at the church he noticed that there were only four people present in the congregation. "Did you tell them I was coming?" he asked the rector. "No" said the rector, "but I'll jolly soon find out who did!"

An absent-minded bishop popped round to a small church in his diocese to hear a newly appointed deacon preach. In the course of his sermon the deacon said, "The most enjoyable days of my life have been spent in the arms of another man's wife." Every member of the congregation sat bolt upright in their seats. After a pause he then said, "My mother." The bishop was impressed by this as a device to keep the congregation interested, so he adopted it in the course of his sermon the following Sunday. "The most enjoyable days of my life have been spent in the arms of another man's wife," he said, to the surprise of the whole Cathedral. Then his mind went blank and he said, "I can't remember her name!"

A bishop received the following note from a vicar in his diocese: "My lord, I regret to inform you of my wife's death. Can you possibly send me a substitute for the weekend?"

One bishop said to another, "I never had sexual intercourse with my wife before I was married. Did you?" "I don't know,", said the other, "what was her maiden name?"

The Dean undressed with heaving breast,
The Bishop's wife to lie on.
He thought it rude to do it nude,
So he kept his old school tie on.

A lonely Jewish man went to Harrods to see if he could buy a Hebrew speaking parrot. He was eventually sold one which could recite the Talmud from beginning to end. He took it home, and opened a book with his friends at the Synagogue that the parrot on the next Sabbath would lead the worship. But it was no good. The parrot never said a word. He took it back home and asked it why it did not speak at the service. "Why did you let me down?" he complained. "Just wait till next Saturday," the parrot replied, "You'll get fantastic odds."

A Rabbi had a direct line to God. He asked God: "In your scale of things what is 60 million years?" God replied, "About a minute." "And," said the Rabbi, "in your scale of things what is £50 million?" "2p", replied God. The Rabbi then said, "O Lord could you let me have 2p?" "Certainly," replied God, "in a minute."

In the course of the church service the vicar happened to notice a lady in the congregation crossing herself and bending the knee whenever in the service mention was made of the devil. Afterwards he happened to meet her at the church door and said to her, "Dear lady, why do you do thus?" to which she replied, "Well, vicar, courtesy costs nothing, and you never know."

A huge flood occurred in the American Mid-West. A man was in a small boat being carried down a wide river. The boat began to sink and a rescue boat approached, but he refused to be rescued, saying, "God will help me." Eventually, as things were getting worse, a helicopter was called, but the man refused to be lifted off, saying the same thing. In the end his boat sank and he drowned. Up he went to heaven and when he met his Maker he said, "Why didn't you help me?" "Well," said God, "I sent a rescue boat and a helicopter, didn't I?"

The Board of Governors of a famous school was interviewing candidates for the shortly to become vacant post of headmaster. The chairman of the governors was a bishop and he was trying to elicit from one candidate his views on how he would run the school. "I would try to encourage the boys to become Christian gentlemen," was the reply. The chairman then asked him, "Would you be kind enough to elaborate a little on that?" "Certainly, my Lord" was the reply, "with which of the two terms is your Lordship unfamiliar?"

A parson had just finished the rehearsal for a wedding ceremony when the bridegroom came back. "Oh vicar," he said, "Will you please be sure to include the word obey in the bride's promise?" "Well", said the parson, "I'm more often asked to leave it out, but I will include it if you want me to." "Oh," said the bridegroom, "I'm not bothered myself, but she wants it in, and I always do what she says!"

A bishop was whiling away the time during a railway journey by doing a crossword puzzle. He leaned across to the man opposite and said, "Could you possibly help me? The clue is "Specifically feminine," and the answer is a four-letter word. I have the last three letters which are "-unt". "Of course," said his companion, "'Aunt' is the answer." "I'm most grateful," said the bishop, "Could you lend me a rubber?"

An Arab banker visiting London was invited to attend a colleague's wedding service at a City church. At the end of the service, which had been conducted in accordance with the 1662 Prayer Book, he said to the priest at the threshold of the church that he had very much enjoyed the service and hoped to return to morning service the following Sunday with his sixteen wives. The parson suggested that it might be thought inappropriate to enter a Christian church with more than one wife. The Arab respectfully replied that the number sixteen seemed to him, having heard the marriage service, to tally with the Christian ideal of "four better, four worse, four richer, four poorer."

A man standing at the Pearly Gates was asked by St Peter the nature of his occupation. "Scrap metal merchant," he replied. "We get very few people of that type here," said St Peter. "In fact I cannot remember when we last had one. I must pop inside and check my Book." When he came out, the scrap metal merchant had gone. So had the Pearly Gates.

AT THE DOCTOR'S

A patient consulted his doctor and said, "Doctor, I've got amnesia." The doctor replied, "How long have you had it?" The patient said, "Had what?" The next patient said, "Doctor, I've got a problem. I can't help my sneezing. I sneeze all the time and every time I sneeze I get a sort of sexual climax." The doctor said, "How interesting. Are you taking anything for this?" The patient replied, "Yes, snuff!"

"Doctor, why is it that the person who snores always goes to sleep first?"

"Doctor, I desperately want to kiss you," said a female patient to her rather attractive medical adviser. "No. No," said the doctor, "That would be quite wrong, and against all my professional rules. I'm not even supposed to be in bed with you."

"You've helped me a lot," said the patient to the psychiatrist as he pointed a gun at him, "but now you know too much."

"I'm troubled about my dreams, doctor," said the young man. "Every night I dream I'm playing cricket for Yorkshire and it's almost my turn to bat." "Just cricket eh?" said the doctor, "Don't you ever dream about girls?" "I daren't, doctor," he replied, "if I did that I'd miss my innings."

Psychiatrist to patient: "Captain Cook circled the globe three times. On which trip did he die?"
Patient: "Give me another example. I'm not very good at history."

Two psychiatrists meet in the street. One says to the other, "You're all right. How am I?"

"My doctor tells me that I shall have to take pills for the rest of my life," said the patient to his friend. "Well, what's your problem?" his friend inquired. "The problem is that he only gave me five."

A barrister worries about what he has left out, a surgeon worries about what he has left in.

A paranoiac thinks two and two makes five; a neurotic knows that two and two make four but is desperately worried about it.

A psychiatrist was being consulted by a patient and as part of his examination he told the patient that he proposed to draw certain shapes and to ask what each of these shapes meant to the patient. The first shape was a square. When asked what this meant to him the patient replied, "sex." The psychiatrist then drew a triangle and a circle and got the same reply to both. He then said to the patient, "I'm afraid you have got sex on the brain." "Come off it," the patient replied, "It's you who's drawing all these filthy pictures."

A lady patient consulted her doctor and when asked what her trouble was she said, "Doctor, when I remove my brassière my breasts do not droop, they rise." The doctor then asked her to remove her bra in order that he might examine her. This she did, and after he had palpated her breasts, he crossed to the window, looked out for a minute or two and then turned and faced her. "Doctor," she said, anxiously, "What have I got?" "Madam," he replied, "I don't know, but I do know that it's infectious."

"Doctor," said a patient on the telephone, "Ten days ago you advised me to run 10 miles a day. I took your advice and I'm now 100 miles from home. What do you advise me to do?"

A man said to his doctor, "Doctor, my wife and I don't get the same satisfaction out of sex that we used to." "What age are you?" asked the doctor. "I'm 81 and she is 79," the man replied. "When did you first notice this?" was the doctor's next question. "Twice last night and once this morning," replied the patient.

A dog-owner discovers that his favourite Alsatian has developed a squint in one eye. He takes the dog to the vet who takes the dog into his surgery and holds him up to the light to take a good look at his eyes in order to diagnose the problem. After a moment or two he says, "I am so sorry, I shall have to put him down." The dog's owner is horrified. "Why?" he asks, "Jip has only got a squint." "I know," gasps the vet, "But he's very very heavy!"

A lady said to her husband, "I went to the doctor this morning, and the doctor told me that I had a very beautiful body." "Oh," said her husband, "and what did the doctor say about your big fat country bum?" "The doctor never mentioned you," she replied.

A man went to a doctor in Harley Street for a physical examination for an insurance policy. The examination began by the doctor asking him questions about his life-style, as he sat opposite the doctor at his desk. "Do you smoke?" was the first question. Answer, "No." "Do you drink alcohol?" was the next question. Answer, "In moderation." Finally, the doctor asked, "And what about sex?" Answer, "Infrequently." The doctor paused for a moment in his writing and then asked, "Is that one word or two?"

Barrister: "Doctor, before you performed the autopsy, did you check for a pulse?"
Doctor: "No."
Barrister: "Did you check the blood pressure?"
Doctor: "No."
Barrister: "Did you check for breathing?"
Doctor: "No".
Barrister: "So, then, it is possible that the patient was alive when you began the autopsy?"
Doctor: "No."
Barrister: "How can you be so sure, doctor."
Doctor: "Because his brain was sitting on my desk in a jar."
Barrister: "But could the patient nevertheless still have been alive?"
Doctor: "It is possible he could have been alive and practising law somewhere."

Overheard in a doctor's waiting room: "I didn't see you here last week, Gladys." "No, deary. I wasn't feeling very well, so I didn't bother coming."

My doctor gives me 15 years of happy retirement, my bank manager only three.

An eye surgeon on his retirement was presented by his colleagues with a huge cast in plastic of an eye. In thanking them most sincerely for the honour, he said, "What a piece of luck I'm not a gynaecologist."

"When I was a houseman I worked under a gynaecologist. He wanted to be a brain surgeon, but he wasn't tall enough."

One of the doctor's patients was a dyslexic atheist who spent the whole of his life denying that there was any kind of dog.

In the USA doctors have a new way of diagnosing a lawyer's health. First, look at his mouth. If it's closed, he's dead.

A doctor was conducting a routine examination of residents in a mental home to ensure that they ought still to be detained. Three patients were in his office. He asked the first, "What is three times three?" He replied, "147." The second was asked the same question and replied, "Thursday." The third was asked the same question and said, "Nine." "How do you work that out?" inquired the doctor. "Easy," was the reply, "147 minus Thursday equals nine.

A heavy drinker consulted his doctor as he was feeling ill. The doctor examined him and then said, "I can't find anything wrong. It must be the drink." "It's all right, doctor," the patient said, "I'll come back when you're sober!".

"I've got malaria," said an elderly patient to his elderly doctor, "I've had it regularly since I was in Palestine in the last war." The doctor examined him and found nothing wrong. He told the patient so. "That's what the doctor in Palestine told me," he said. "Which unit were you with. With the --- Fusiliers," he said. "The doctor replied, "So was I. I was the regimental doctor and I was the doctor who examined you." "No," said the patient, "That can't be right. He was much younger than you."

THE FAIR SEX

During the Second War a young naval officer was sitting at the bar of Shepheard's Hotel in Cairo when, towards the end of the evening, a frog suddenly appeared at the end of the bar. This in itself was surprising, but the frog could also speak and said, "I am not really a frog as you might suppose. I am a very very attractive girl, but I can only regain my human form if I am taken over water. Can you help me?" The naval officer was amazed and did not for a moment believe what was being said, but it was late at night and he put the frog in his jacket pocket and drove himself back to his ship at Alexandria. There he went on board, and when he got to his cabin he put the frog on his bunk and to his utter amazement the frog turned into a most beautiful young lady ... "And that my lord, is the case for the defence."

Behind every successful man there is an ambitious wife and an astonished mother-in-law.

Adam was walking round the Garden of Eden feeling a little lonely, so God asked Adam, "What is wrong with you?" Adam replied that he didn't have anyone to talk to. God said he planned to give him a companion and it would be a woman. God said, "This person will cook for you and wash your clothes, she will always agree with every decision you make. She will bear your children and never ask you to get up in the middle of the night to take care of them. She will not nag you, and will always be the first to admit that she was wrong when you've had a disagreement. She will never have a headache and will always give you love and compassion whenever needed." Adam asked God, "What will a woman like this cost?" God replied, "An arm and a leg." Adam replied, "What can I get for just a rib?" The rest is history.

A couple married on May 1 and separated on May 2. "What happened?" asked the lawyer. "Oh, we just gradually drifted apart," was the answer.

An angry wife met her husband at the door. There was alcohol on his breath and lipstick on his collar. "I assume," she snarled, "that there is a very good reason for you to come waltzing in here at six o'clock in the morning." "There is," he replied, "Breakfast."

"Darling!" said the wife, "The car won't start. I think there's some water in the carburettor." "How do you know?" said the husband, "You don't know anything about car engines." "Darling," replied the wife, "The car's in the canal."

Under a former Matrimonial Causes Act a spouse who had committed adultery was obliged to put in a disclosure of such adultery in the form of what was known as a Discretion Statement. This was sealed, and opened by the judge who considered it in deciding whether or not to grant a decree of divorce. Many passages in such statements are memorable. Here are two:

"I associated with John Smith for many years and committed adultery with him at my home and various other places. I was sorry when it was over."

"I didn't know what adultery was until I met my solicitor."

Canadian scientists recently suggested that men should take look at their beer consumption, since the results of a recent analysis revealed the presence of female hormones in beer. The theory is that drinking beer makes men turn into women. To test this finding 100 men were fed eight pints of beer each. It was then observed that 100 per cent of the men gained weight, talked excessively without making sense, became overly emotional, couldn't drive, failed to think rationally, argued over nothing, and refused to apologise when wrong. No further testing is planned.

"Hey," said a lady to a male guest at a drinks party, "You look a lot like my third husband." "Really, madam," was the reply, "how many husbands have you had?" "Two," she replied.

"Women are like tricks by sleight of hand,
Which to admire we should not understand."

A man was approached in a supermarket by a very smart lady who asked him about his health, his job, and his new house. The man was obviously puzzled and she said, "You clearly don't know me." "The face is familiar," the man replied, "but the name escapes me." "I am your first wife," she said.

In the words of Groucho Marx, if you want to be a Duchess, be a Duchess. If you want to make love - hats off.

My wife has run off with my next door neighbour. I do miss him!

A young lady on the beach at St Juan-les-Pins was wearing a T-shirt bearing the legend, "I am a virgin." Underneath in very small letters was printed the PS: "This is a very old T-shirt."

When I married I said to my wife, "If ever I'm unfaithful to you, I'll buy you a bunch of flowers." In the course of a very happy marriage I've saved myself a lot of money.

As I drove in to work today on the motorway I looked over my left shoulder and saw a woman overtaking me on the inside with her face close to her rear-view mirror, putting on make-up. She veered half-way into my lane. It scared me so badly I almost dropped my battery shaver into my coffee.

General Mark Clark was asking a young officer, "What is the best piece of advice you've ever received?" "Get married," was the reply. "Who gave it to you?" asked the General. "My wife," the young man replied.

The scene is the deep south of the USA. A man carrying a pig, a chicken and a pail stopped a woman and asked her the way to X. She told him, but said, "Of course there's a short cut through the woods, but I wouldn't dare show you that in case you ... in case you ... took advantage of me." The man replied, "What! With all this on me?" She said, "Oh, that wouldn't matter, you could put the pig in the pail and I'd hold the chicken!"

"You only married me because Aunt Mabel left me a quarter of a million." "Rubbish! I would have married you whoever left you the money."

In divorce proceedings your wife will take you for every penny she can get; your solicitor for every penny she can't.

A psychiatrist asks a lot of expensive questions which your wife asks you for nothing.

A pessimist thinks all women are bad. The optimist hopes they will be.

Barrister to lady journalist in El Vino's bar in Fleet Street, a favourite haunt of lawyers and newsmen: "I want to make love to you." The journalist replied, "If you were to make love to me I should undoubtedly hear about it."

The wife is in bed with her lover when her husband returns. If he walks away, that is *savoir faire*. If he listens at the bedroom door and stays in the house, that is *laisser faire*. If he goes into the bedroom, that is *sang froid*.

In life there are three statements never to believe: (1) the cheque is in the post, (2) Darling, I'll still love you just as much in the morning, and (3) I'm from the government and I'm here to help you.

"I can read my wife like a book."
"What's your system?"
"Braille!"

A couple sitting in a restaurant seemed to be having a wonderful time. But as the woman glanced away from the table, their waiter rushed over. "Madam" he said,"Your husband has just slid under the table!" "No, he hasn't," she replied,"My husband has just come through the door."

"I was brought up in another age - and not the Third Age either," said the senior member of a London club, "When a joint was what we put in the oven, a pot was what we cooked it in, and going all the way meant taking a bus to the depot!"

"Let me buy you a Rolls Royce," said the husband to his wife. "I don't want a Rolls Royce," she replied. "Well let me buy you a diamond necklace ... a flat on the Riviera." "I don't want any of these things," she said. "Well what do you want?" he asked. "I want a divorce," she said. "Oh," was the reply, "I hadn't thought of spending that much!"

Two City gents were fishing the Oykell in remote Ross-shire. Darkness fell, the rain began, and they had had no luck, so they started back to their car. Unhappily they got lost, but they spotted the light of a small cottage to which they went and were invited in by the charming lady occupant. She insisted they have supper and dry their clothes and stay the night. Nine months later one gent rang the other and said, "You remember the night we spent with that charming lady on the Oykell?" "Yes. I do." "Well did you by any chance visit her room in the course of the night?" "As a matter of fact I did!" "And did you by any chance in the course of your visit give her my name?" "I'm sorry old boy, I did. I do apologise." "Not to worry," said the other, "she just died and left me two million pounds."

One should always be astute, even in moments of crisis, to use the right word. An example of this is said to be the Professor of English who was discovered by his wife in bed with another woman. "I am surprised," said she. "No, my dear," said her husband, "We were surprised. You were astonished."

Misprints do occur in newspapers and even in personal correspondence, where we are all from time to time guilty of what are sometimes called Freudian slips. Among the latter was a postcard on a business trip from a husband to his wife, "Having a wonderful time. Wish you were her." And among the former a report of a wedding which ran: "The happy couple departed for an unknown destination where the honeymoney will be spent."

Attractive lady barrister to respondent husband in the witness box on the hearing of wife's petition for nullity of marriage on the ground of non-consummation: "Mr Johnson, I have to suggest to you that you are impotent." Witness: "You come outside with me, young lady, and I'll prove you wrong."

A man and a girl were sitting in a car on some waste ground very late at night. The car was seen by a police officer who approached it and saw the man reading a newspaper and the girl doing her knitting. "'Allo, 'Allo," he said, "what's going on?" "We're waiting, officer," said the man, "She'll be sixteen in 10 minutes' time."

A husband and wife are lying in bed. The husband asks the wife, "Did you fake that last night?" She replies, "No. I really was asleep!"

Customer in pet shop to young assistant: "Can I have a parrot for my wife?" Assistant: "Sorry, sir. We don't do swaps."

"Do you ever kiss on your first date?"
"No, of course not."
"Well, do you ever kiss on your second date?"
"I never had a second date."

Mixed feelings is what a man has when he sees his mother-in-law driving over a cliff in his brand new car.

A Texan staying in the Waldorf Astoria Hotel in New York was bitterly complaining that this was not a first-class hotel. "In Texas in a first-class hotel, they come around to your room at midnight and they holler out, "Have you got a woman in there?" and if you say, "No," why, they throw one in."

A man was kneeling in a cemetery beside a well-kept grave. A bystander felt so sorry for him, and approached him saying very sympathetically, "My poor man, who are you grieving for? Your parents? Your brother?" "No," he replied, "For my wife's first husband!"

An elderly man was sitting on a bench in Park Square, Leeds, weeping uncontrollably. A barrister on his way to chambers, approached him, and asked if he could help, and why was he weeping. "I'm 83 today," he said, "and two months ago I wed a most lovely lady of 29. She's good looking, she cooks beautifully, and we have sex twice every night." "Well," said the barrister, "why are you crying?" He replied, "Because I can't remember where I live!"

Two elderly gentlemen were sitting in the same Square, when a most attractive young lady walked past. One man said to the other "Jim, do you remember when we was in the army and they give us them bromide tablets to take our minds off sex?" "Aye, I do," said his companion. "Well, Jim," said the first man, "I think mine are wearing off."

Two nuns went into town in a red Austin Mini. One dropped the other at the shopping area to do the shopping and they arranged to meet later. The first nun went to the pre-arranged place but there was no sign of her friend, so she asked a passer-by whether he had seen a nun in a red Mini. "I'm afraid I haven't," he said, "but nowadays nothing would surprise me."

Housewife to Bridget, the home help: "Bridget, the dust is so thick I can write my name on the piano." "Oh ma'am, what it is to have the education."

A TV station was conducting a market research survey to ascertain the reasons for long life among elderly persons. The first man who was asked to what he attributed his long life replied: "I'm 83 and I've 'ad a bottle of whisky each day, and two on Sundays." The second replied, "I'm 91 and I've smoked 50 cigarettes a day and a cigar on Sundays." The third replied: "Sexual intercourse twice a day every day and three times on Sundays." When asked his age he replied, "27."

The *bon mots* attributed to Mae West are legion, but it seems that these are among the pick of the crop:
"Too much of a good thing can be wonderful."
"I generally avoid temptation, unless I can't resist it."
"When I'm good, I'm very very good, but when I'm bad I'm better."
"It's better to be looked over than overlooked."
Boy friend: "Your lips, your teeth, your eyes, your hair, your ..."
Mae West: "Say, what are you doing, making love or stocktaking?"

"How is your relationship going?" "Like clockwork. My wife keeps winding me up!"

A social worker was visiting a single mother living in Bethnal Green. She had six children and the social worker asked their names. "They're all called Wayne," said the mother. "Doesn't that cause difficulties?" asked the social worker. "No. It makes it easy," said the mother, "If I wants 'em to come in I just shouts 'Wayne!' and they all come running." "But suppose," said the social worker, "Suppose you just want one of them?" "Oh then I use their surnames," replied the mother.

LITTLE ONES

A Swiss Cottage school-teacher reported that while she was giving a French lesson to her class of 11-year olds she pointed to a fly on the ceiling and said, "There is a fly. "Can anyone tell me how to say that in French?" "Voici le mouche," said a boy in the front row. "No, Peter," said she. "Not 'le mouche.' It's 'la mouche'." The boy gave her an innocent smile, "Crumbs!" he said, "what super eyesight!"

On the first day of school, the kindergarten teacher said, "If anyone wants to go to the lavatory, hold up your hand." A little voice from the back of the room said, "Please, miss, how will that help?"

Three little boys, one English, one French and one Swiss, were talking together. The English boy said, "I know how babies come. They are brought by the stork." The French boy said, "No. That is wrong. How they come has something to do with sex." The Swiss boy said, "You are both wrong; it varies from canton to canton."

Old boy to absent-minded schoolmaster, "My brother and I were both here at the school. Do you remember us?" "Yes, of course I do," was the reply, "but which of you was killed in the war?"

Many years ago a country doctor was called out by a patient in labour. She lived in a remote part of the county - so remote that there was no electricity in the house, and when he arrived there was no-one at home except for the expectant mother and her five year-old child. The doctor asked the child to hold up an oil lamp while the doctor did what was necessary. The boy complied, and the baby in due course was delivered. The doctor lifted him by his feet and spanked his bottom to help him take his first breath. He then asked the five year-old what he thought of the baby. "Hit him again," said the little boy, "He had no business crawling up there in the first place!"

The daughter of the family woke up one morning and made it quite plain to her parents that she did not want to go to school. "I'm fed up with school," she said. "I'm bored. I don't like the buildings. I don't like the people. I'm browned off." Her mother said, "Darling, you've got to go to school. You can't stay at home. You've got to go to school, first because you've got to go, and second because you're the headmistress."

A small boy tells his mother, very proudly, that he has been chosen to play a part in his form's Christmas play. When she asks him what part he replies, "A piece of paper." This mysterious answer is only cleared up by another parent who tells the mother that her son is to be a page.

The time came round for the annual school play, and this year it was to be Shakespeare. The plot required the boys to wear tights. Matron saw the master-in-charge and expressed her view that it would only be decent if under their tights they all wore jockstraps. The master agreed, and relayed this information to the boys, whereupon one of them said, "Sir, does that apply to boys with small parts?"

The parents of a small boy at boarding school were not able to attend the school play, which was a performance of *Hamlet*. The boy's letter to his parents that weekend read: "Most of the parents had seen it before, but they laughed just the same."

A small boy at a preparatory school had his height measured in the usual way and his report said: "His height at beginning of term 5'1." Height at end of term 5'0." The form master's comments read: "This term Andrew has settled down nicely."

A school report said: "James's handwriting has greatly improved this term." What his form master wanted to add was, "Now that we can read his writing, we realise what an ill-educated boy he is."

A small boy arrived home early from school one afternoon and was asked by his father why he had come back so early. "I was sent home, pa," he said, "for peeing in the pool." "Why son, everybody pees in the pool." The boy replied, "Is that right, dad? From the top board?"

A French lady was showing her two small girls round the Paris Zoo, and by-and-by they arrived at the elephant house. There happened to be an elephant with an enormous erection. When the small girls saw this, one of them said to her mother, "Maman, qu'est que c'est au milieu de l'éléphant?" Her mother, slightly embarrassed, replied, "Ah, chérie, c'est rien du quoi, rien du quoi." The keeper standing near by, overheard this remark and said to himself in a stage whisper, "Ah, comment madame est blasé."

A small boy, lunching with his mother in a high class restaurant, left a delicious steak uneaten. His mother wrapped it up in her napkin, popped it into her bag, and said, in the hearing of the other customers, "We will give this to the dog." "Oh, good, mummy," said her son, "Are we going to get a dog?"

A mother said to her small daughter, "Run along to the butcher's shop and see if he has pig's feet." Half an hour later the daughter returned and said, "I couldn't tell, he had shoes on."

A staid looking gentleman was upset at the dress of some young people in the street. "Just look at that one," he barked to a bystander. "Is it a boy or a girl?" "It's a girl. She's my daughter." "Do forgive me," apologised the man,"I didn't know you were her mother." "I'm not," snapped the bystander, "I'm her father."

Seven-year old Timothy was late home for tea, and his mother was rather cross. "Where have you been until this time?" she wanted to know. "I've been watching a bicycle race," he replied. "Oh, and who won?" asked mother with a glimmer of interest. "A man," replied Timothy. "Well," said mother, "I didn't expect it would be a monkey." "No," replied Timothy solemnly, "the monkey came second."

Cliff Morgan used to say that he learnt a lot of things at Sunday School. One was that the Epistles were not the wives of the Apostles.

A grandmother was asked to look at her daughter's new-born baby. Holding it in her arms she said, "Is it a boy or a girl?" "Oh, mother!" her daughter said, "You need glasses." "No," said granny, "It isn't my eyesight, it's my memory."

A small boy was asked by his teacher to write an essay on the law. It contained the phrase, "The police is bastards". The teacher was very concerned, and arranged a visit to the local police station where the young man was received warmly and given cups of tea and cake. In his next essay appeared the phrase, "The police is cunning bastards".

A little girl aged three was talking to a friend of her parents and said with a complete lack of enthusiasm, "Mummy and Daddy and I are flying to Paris." "That should be fun," said the friend. After they returned the friend saw the little girl again and asked how she got on. "It was lovely," she said, "We didn't fly, we went by aeroplane."

Lecturing her six-year old son on morals, a mother concluded: "Always remember, son, we're in this world to help others." "Yes, mum," her son replied, "and what are the others here for?"

An even younger little girl saw her father putting on his dinner jacket before leaving for an official function. "Daddy," she said, "why are putting on that black and white suit again? You know it always gives you a headache in the morning."

A little girl saw her grandfather putting vodka in his morning orange juice. "Don't you realise that what you're doing means a slow death?" she said. "Who's in a hurry?" he replied.

The moral of this story is that it is always unwise to under-estimate the intelligence of your audience. A young schoolteacher in Hackney decided to try to broaden his experience, so he applied for a post in North Yorkshire and was posted to Whitby. On his first day, confronted by a class of eight year-olds, he decided to give them a general intelligence test, and put on the blackboard various pictures. Without exception they all recognised an aeroplane and a cruise-ship. His next picture was that of a sheep. When this picture went up there was a deafening silence. "Come along, come along," said the teacher, "You live in the country. You must all know the name of this animal." There was no response, but after a long interval Tommy in the front row put up his hand. "Yes. Tommy," said the teacher. "I think ... said Tommy, "I think ... its a well-formed unsheared gimmer out of a Border Leicester ewe crossed with a Lincoln Longwool tup ... and it looks to me like one of Joe Riley's!"

A bishop was asked to give away the prizes at a local girls' school. One of the prizes was to the girl who was most likely to do well in life. When the bishop handed her this prize he said to her, in an effort to say the right thing, "And what are you going to do when you leave school?" Her reply was, "Well, I had thought of going straight home!"

A mother sent a note to school with her small boy. This read: "Johnny has swallowed 50p. If there's no change on Monday we'll take him to the doctor!"

A friend telephoned and a hoarse quiet voice answered. "Who is that?" he asked. "It's James," was the whispered reply. "Are your mummy or daddy in?" "Yes, they're upstairs. They're busy." "Well, is your brother there?" "Yes, he's in the garage, he's busy." "Would grandma be available?" "She's busy too. She's in the garden." "Well, could you ask your mummy or daddy to come to the phone?" "No, they're talking to a policeman." "What are they all doing?" Answer in a hoarse whisper, "They're looking for me!"

The following appeared in two 12 year old's history examination papers: "The greatest writer of the Renaissance was William Shakespeare. He was born in the year 1564, supposedly on his birthday. He never made much money and is famous only because of his plays. He wrote tragedies, comedies, and hysterectomies, all in Islamic pentameters. Romeo and Juliet are examples of a heroic couple. Romeo's last wish was to be laid by Juliet." "Writing at the same time as Shakespeare was Miguel Cervantes. He wrote *Donkey Hote*. The next great author was John Milton. Milton wrote *Paradise Lost*. Then his wife died and he wrote *Paradise Regained*."

Barrister to child in the witness box: "What school did you go to? All your responses must be oral."
Child: "Oral."

A man was blessed with twin sons, and could not tell them apart. In an effort to make them different each was sent to a different prep. school, a different public school, and a different University - one to Oxford, one to Cambridge. The one at Oxford came back a typical Oxford gentleman, the one at Cambridge a typical Cambridge drunkard. And he still couldn't tell them apart!

ON THE BALL

When asked why Northern Ireland always did so well on the soccer field, Danny Blanchflower replied, "We always put in an equalizer before the other side get a chance to score."

Johnny Williams, of Harlequins and England, was playing in Paris for Harlequins, the game being refereed by a Frenchman who spoke little English. Williams had been penalised several times for a crooked feed to the scrum. Finally, when penalised again, he in exasperation invited the referee to "get stuffed." To this the referee replied, "the apology is too late."

A 70 year-old was seen in the car park at Twickenham before an International with a girl on each arm. One of his friends said to him, "At your age, Jim?!" His reply was, "In the old days it was pure pleasure; now it's to keep me up."

Dr Tommy Kemp tells how, when he was at St Mary's Hospital, he was anxious to recruit X to strengthen the hospital rugby XV. The governing body insisted that, however good a candidate's rugby, he had to undergo an oral examination and have a pass rate of 50 per cent. X appeared for his oral and Dr Kemp asked two questions: (1) "What is the colour of blue litmus paper?" X said red, so that was wrong. (2) "Do you know how to make sulphuric acid?" X said No. That was right, and he was in.

In the words of Ray Prosser, speaking of the celebrated Colin Meads, the All Black forward, the distinctive feature of his play on the rugby field was the terminal traces of your jock-strap in his mouth at the conclusion of each game.

A rugby player decided to emigrate to Australia and went along to Australia House to inquire about the form. He there saw a clerk who sat him down at a desk and said to him, "Tell me, cobber, have yew got any previous convictions?" "I didn't know you still needed them for Australia," he replied.

Every wing forward is born just ever so slightly off-side.

Max Beerbohm defined a rowing eight as eight men with but a single thought - if that.

A French front-row forward left the field after an energetic international rugby game against England at the Stade de France, covered in blood with a broken nose. He was asked later what he thought of the game and he replied, "C'est virile, mais c'est correcte."

Fred Trueman's father is alleged to have said to Fred when he was a young man, "Now then, Fred, if you're not in bed by 10, come straight home."

On a Saturday afternoon a wife returned from shopping, knowing that her husband would have been watching the football on the TV. "What was the score, darling?" she asked. "Nil-nil," he replied. "What was the score at half-time?" she asked. "I don't know," he said, "I only watched the second half."

To sport and to recognise a club tie is a deeply ingrained English habit, but from time to time mistakes do arise. A young undergraduate was elected to the Hawks Club of Cambridge University, a club restricted to those members of the University who have displayed outstanding games or athletic prowess. He was told that the tie would be recognised the world over and would always be the catalyst which secured an introduction to fellow members. He found this build-up very impressive. A few days later he was standing in a bus queue in London and the man standing next to him said, "`Ere. Nice to see you wearing the tie!" "Yes, indeed," said the young man. "`Old on a minute," said his companion. "I can't place your face. How long 'ave you bin a member of the Balham and Tooting Cycling Club?"

A Scotsman appeared at the Pearly Gates and was asked by St Peter why he thought he should be admitted. "I've been guid to my wife and children," he replied. "That's common enough," replied Peter, "but is there anything outstanding?" "Aye," said the Scot, "I went to the Celtic and Rangers game, stood among the Rangers and shouted, "Well played, Celtic." "Yes, that was very brave," said Peter, "When was this?" "Aboot three minutes ago," was the reply.

An atheist is a man who can watch Rangers and Celtic playing football without caring who wins.

Trueman was batting for England in Calcutta, and was given out lbw. He left the pitch and as he did so he said to a man in a white coat, "You want your eyes examining." The man replied, "So do you, sahib, I'm only selling ice-cream!"

Arthur Wood, the Yorkshire wicket-keeper, was playing for England in a pre-war Test match at the Oval against Australia. He went out to bat when England were 600 for 6. "Good luck Arthur," shouted someone on the terraces. "Aye," he shouted back, "I'm just the man for a crisis."

An international rugby referee died and went to the Pearly Gates where he was asked whether during his time on earth he was aware of having committed any particular sin. "Yes," he replied, "In an international where Wales were playing England I awarded Wales a try after a forward pass." "That is not a matter of any consequence," he was told, "Please come in." "Thank you St Peter," he said. "Oh, I'm not St Peter," said the guardian angel, "He's on holiday, I'm St David."

One golfer said to another: "Good Lord, Frank! There's my wife playing a round of golf with my mistress." "You took the words right out of my mouth," his friend replied.

Two dedicated golfers were playing a round together. A hearse went by and one of them raised his hat. "Why are you doing that?" his companion asked. "Well, I've been married 19 years, and that's the least I can do for the wife," he replied.

"The other night," said the addictive golfer, "my wife shouted at me 'Golf! Golf! Golf! That's all you ever think about - Golf.' This frightened the life out of me - well after all you don't expect anyone on the fourteenth green at that time of night."

A man who was an addictive golfer and who was getting on in years, consulted a spiritualist in order to discover, when the fateful time arrived, whether he could play golf in heaven or, as he liked to think of it, in the Elysian fields. The reply to his query was: "I have for you both good news and bad news. Which would you like first?" The golfer chose the good news, and the lady said, "The good news is that in heaven there is the best golf course you could ever imagine . It puts St Andrew's in the shade." "But what is the bad news?" inquired the golfer. "The bad news is," she said, "that you are due on the first tee on Monday next at 7 am."

The one occasion on which it is said that President Wilson smiled was when he was playing golf with his wife. She took a 6-iron for her second shot at the long fourth and said to the caddy, "Will I get to the green with this?" "Sure you will," he replied, "if you use it often enough."

When Bob Hope returned to the clubhouse at Wentworth Park, someone asked him how he got on and he replied, "If you want to know why I took four putts at the 18th, it's because I like putting."

George was a life-long golfer whose eyesight began to fail as he got into his sixties. He consulted the family doctor who mentioned the name of a much older man who had perfect eyesight and might be able to help him. So George went along to see Arthur who confirmed that although his memory was bad, he had sight like an eagle, and would gladly come along to the golf course and act as watcher. This seemed to George a great idea. So off they went, and on the first tee George drove a respectable 200 yards, but of course lost the direction of the ball. He asked Arthur, "Did you see my shot?" to which Arthur replied, "I certainly did." "Where did it go?" he asked. Arthur replied, "I forget."

A couple were playing golf one day on the most exclusive course in Surrey. The third tee ran near some very expensive houses, and the husband said to his wife, "Watch your tee shot darling. If we break one of those windows they'll take us to the cleaners." His wife pulled her drive and it went straight through a ground floor window. They decided the best course was to go and apologise, so they walked to the door, rang the bell and heard a voice say, "Come in." In they went, and there on the floor was broken glass and the remains of a broken bottle. In an armchair was a man who said, "If you are the people who broke my window, I want to thank you. I am a genie who was trapped in that bottle for a thousand years. Now that I'm released I can grant three wishes. You can have one each and I'll keep the last for myself." "Marvellous," said the husband, "I'd like a million pounds a year for life." "No problem," said the genie, "It's the least I can do. And what is your wish?" he said to the wife. "I want a house in every Caribbean island," she replied. "Consider it done," the genie replied. "And what's your wish, genie?" said the husband. "Well, I haven't had sex with a woman for a thousand years and my wish is to sleep with your wife." The couple looked at each other. The husband said, "Well, we did get a load of stuff, darling, how about it, I don't mind." So the couple go upstairs to the bedroom and after two hours of pleasure the genie says to the wife, "And how old is your husband?" "He's 35," she replied. "And he still believes in genies" said her companion, "... that's amazing!"

IN THE AIR

An aircraft was fully automated and to give the passengers confidence this was explained to them as the plane was taking off. The message they heard on the tannoy was, "We are now taking off. This aircraft is fully and efficiently automated. There is therefore no cabin crew and meals will be served automatically. All you have to do is to sit back and enjoy the flight flight flight flight."

Soon after the Second War a distinguished pilot and holder of the Air Force Cross, was talking to sixth formers about his wartime experiences. The chairman of the meeting was, of course, the headmaster. The pilot was describing an air battle over France, and said, "There were six Fokkers to starboard and six Fokkers to port, all coming out of the sun." The chairman rose and explained, "Fokker is of course the name of a continental aircraft." "That's very true, chairman," said the pilot, "but these Fokkers were Messerschmitts."

A porter, loaded down with suitcases, followed the couple to the airline check-in desk. As they approached the queue, the husband glanced at the pile of luggage and said to his wife, "Why didn't you bring the piano too?" "Are you trying to be funny?" she demanded. "No," he sighed, "I left the tickets on it."

An elderly lady with her dog in a basket was about to board an aircraft. She was told that the dog must go in the hold. In the end she agreed, but asked that he be taken great care of. At the end of the flight it was discovered by the baggage handlers that the dog was dead. They informed the staff who, with great efficiency, procured another dog of similar type which they placed in the basket. This was delivered to the passenger, but when she opened it she said, "That's not my dog! My dog was dead."

During the Gulf War, General Schwartzkop was briefing his pilots. "Fly to Baghdad at 10,000 feet, drop your bombs, and fly back to base," he said. One of the pilots asked, "Say we fly in at 8,000 feet?" The General replied, "When you get home you'll get a purple heart." Another pilot asked, "Say we fly in at 5,000 feet?" "If you get home," said the General, "you'll get a purple heart with clusters and a letter of commendation from the President of the USA." The final question was, "Say we fly in at 2,000 feet?" "No," said the General, "I wouldn't recommend that. At that height you could bump into those sons of bitches from the RAF."

A Boeing 737 on a long haul flight was stacked over Heathrow. After several minutes of circling the captain radioed Air Traffic Control and said, "I'm running out of fuel. Can you please give me emergency priority to land?" Control replied, "What's your endurance?" The Captain replied (after a puzzled pause), "Well I'm with the Scottish Widows, and the 737 is with Lloyds of London."

An American lady staying in London was planning a trip to France, and rang the British Airways information desk to inquire about flight times. The clerk at the information desk answered the telephone and the lady said, "Can you tell me how long it would take to fly from London to Paris?" "Just a minute madam," the clerk replied. "Oh," said the customer, putting the phone down, "I thought it took longer than that."

It is, or is said to be, a fact of musical life that men with tenor voices are slightly thick. This is supported by the case of the rotund Italian tenor in the boarding queue at Heathrow with an economy ticket for a flight to New York. Having boarded the plane he sat in the very front row of business class where his girth was so enormous and his belongings so numerous that no other passenger could get past him. The lady flight attendant approached him and suggested he move to the back of the plane as he was being an obstruction and in any event was in the wrong seat. He refused and continued to refuse when approached by the senior flight attendant, who as a result consulted the captain of the aircraft. The captain went straight up to the man and whispered something in his ear, whereupon without a word he went to the back of the plane. Loading was completed, and after the plane took off, the senior flight attendant said to the captain, "What did you say to that guy to get him to move his seat so quickly?" The captain replied, "Oh! I simply told him that the part of the plane where he was sitting did not go to New York."

One of the passengers happened to be a large soprano from the deep South. She was obviously having great difficulty in getting down the aisle because of her girth, so the flight attendant said to her, "Madam might find it easier if she turned sideways," to which the singer replied, "Honey, I don't have no sideways!"

A parachutist was doing a jump, but unfortunately when he pulled the release cord, the chute failed to open and he plunged towards the ground. On the way down he passed another man going up to whom he shouted, "Know anything about parachutes?" The other man replied, "No! Know anything about gas stoves?"

ON PARADE

Australia is one million square miles of Sergeants' Mess.

At the same table on a train were three Brigadiers and a Sergeant Major. The Brigadiers were talking of their families and boasting about the achievements of their sons. One of them, as a matter of politeness, asked the Sergeant Major if he had any family. "I'm not married," he replied, "but I've got three sons and they're all Brigadiers."

A conversation between two radio operators went as follows:
"Hello 149, advise you to change course 20 degrees to port, over."
"Hello 150, advise *you* to change course, over."
Pause.
"Hello 150. You are on a collision, repeat collision, course. Change course forthwith, over."
"Hello 149, it is *you* who should change course, over."
"Hello 150, this is the United States Navy Aircraft Carrier John F. Kennedy, change course forthwith or counter-measures will be taken to secure the safety of this vessel, over."
"Hello 149, this is the light-house, over."

The drill sergeant said to his recruits before their first weekend leave, "You horrible creatures! If you want it you'll find it. If you find it you'll get it. And if you get it you've had it!"

A new computer was installed in the Pentagon. It was fully programmed, and details of a hypothetical battle situation were fed in. The next question was, "Should the US Army advance or retreat?" Its answer was, "Yes." The next question was, "Yes what?" Back came the answer, "Yes, Sir."

Lord Bingham tells of an incident involving General Sedgwick at the Battle of the Wilderness (1864) during the American Civil War. The General was visiting a front-line unit and was told by the local commander not to put his body above the earthworks because there were snipers about. "Snipers," said the General as he raised himself above the trench and looked about him. "Those guys can't shoot. They couldn't hit an elephant at this dist ... dist ... dist."

PICK AND MIX

A wealthy man was picked up at the airport by his chauffeur. "How are things James?" he asked. "Well, do you want the good news or the bad news?" replied the chauffeur. "Bad news first please," said his employer. "Well the dog is dead," he replied. "That happened because he was kicked by the quietest horse in the stable. The quiet horse was disturbed by an ember from the burning stable roof. The thatch on the stable caught fire because the big house was burnt down, and the big house caught fire because a candle on your wife's coffin tipped over. Oh, I forgot - your wife is dead." "After all that, what's the good news?" asked his employer. "The good news is that the heat of the fire has made the daffodils come up two weeks early."

A friend once said to Frank Crozier, "What are you doing for Christmas? I expect you will be surrounded by your nearest and dearest," to which he replied, "No, just at home with the wife and children."

An Englishman, a Frenchman and a Russian were describing the happiest moment of their lives. The Englishman said that it was his return from work at the end of the day to find his slippers by the fire, newspaper on the table, and a glass of whisky by his side. The Frenchman said that for him it was two weeks in the sun at Cannes with his mistress. The Russian said: "It is 3 am. I am in bed with my wife. There is a knock at the door of my flat. I answer it and there is the KGB who say to me, "Alexei Alexeivitch you are under arrest." Then for me it is the happiest moment of my life when I say to the KGB, "Alexei Alexeivitch, he live next door!"

A Chinese immigrant to the UK saw the advertisement. "Go to work on an egg." So he bought an egg, put it in his garage, joined the AA and went to work on it. One day it would not start, so he rang the AA. The man there was a bit puzzled, but eventually said, "Why don't you try pulling out the yoke.?" A few minutes later the Chinaman rang back and said, "I did what you suggested. It's all white now."

A man asked Bob Hope what happened if a snake bit him. "Well, you suck it out," replied Bob. "But what if it's in a place you can't reach?" his friend asked. "That's when you know who your friends are," said Bob.

"I used to use a lot of clichés, but now I avoid them like the plague."

As one drunkard said to another, "You must stop drinking, your face is getting blurred!"

What is the difference between a carpet, an egg and sex. The answer is that you can beat a carpet, you can beat an egg, but you can't beat sex.

A man in Moscow visited a car dealer and ordered a new car. He was told that delivery would be 10 years from that day. "Will it be morning or afternoon?" he inquired. When asked by the dealer whether it mattered, he said, "Yes it does matter because the plumber is coming in the morning!"

On his first visit to the Athenaeum Club, Sir James Barrie asked an octogenarian biologist the way to the coffee room. The biologist burst into tears. He had been a member for 50 years. No one had spoken to him before.

The distinguished families of Boston Massachusetts are the Lowells, the Lodges and the Cabots. A well-connected visitor was walking back to his hotel in Boston one night when he happened to see Felicity Cabot soliciting for business. "Whatever brought you to this?" he asked. "Well," she said, "it was either this or dipping into capital."

As Lech Walesa once said, "You can only be certain of one thing in this life, and by then it's too late - they are screwing the coffin lid on."

You may be able to remember the newly appointed radio announcer on the Home Service who said, "It is 9 o'clock Greenwich. Meantime here is the news." His experience was not dissimilar to that of the disc jockey who dedicated a record, "to Mrs Jackson who is 111" ... "I'm sorry," he added, "I should have said to Mrs Jackson who is ill."

Things are pretty casual down under. At an official dinner in Sydney, a waiter served the butter and a guest asked, "May I have another pat." "No," said the waiter, "my orders are one guest, one pat." "Do you know who I am?" asked the guest, "I'm the captain of the cricket club of New South Wales." "Do you know who I am?" asked the waiter. "No," said the guest. " Well, cobber, I'm the guy with the butter."

One business man said to another, "There's only one honest way of making money. Do you know what it is?" The other replied, "I've no idea." "I thought not," was the reply.

A husband died, and his coffin had to be carried a little way over a rough track between the hearse and the grave. The pall bearers stumbled and the coffin broke open. To the astonishment of all present, including the grieving widow, the husband emerged from the coffin as large as life. Two years later he died again, and as the coffin approached the same spot the wife said, "Take special care at this point."

Mr Gulbenkian was asked if he had a family motto. He replied, "Service ... and my God I get it." When asked by a passport official at London Airport, "What is your position?" he replied, "Enviable."

A father was explaining to his son the difference between annoyance, anger and frustration. "If you telephone any number at random and say, 'Is Mick there?' that will produce annoyance. If you ring the same number again and ask the same question, that produces anger. But if you ring the same number and say, 'Hello, Mick here! Any messages for me?' that is guaranteed to produce frustration."

Logic is to be found everywhere. Even with an old lady who said to a booking clerk, "Can I have a return ticket please?" The clerk said, "Where to?" and she replied, "Here of course."

Farmer's wife to husband, "What was the name of those pills we gave the bull to improve his performance?" "I can't remember," her husband replied, "But I know they tasted of peppermint."

Man: "I had to leave my aerobics class because I broke a toe."
Friend: "How is it?"
Man: "I don't know, it wasn't my toe."

On his way to work in Wall Street, New York, a young man put a quarter into a pretzel machine outside a paper shop for a whole year, but never took a pretzel from the machine. After a year he put in his quarter as usual, and was about to walk away, when the shopkeeper came running out. "I know what you're going to say," he said. "No," she replied, "You're wrong. I was going to tell you the price has gone up."

A Northern business manager flew off to a conference in Florida and wanted to send his wife an e-mail to say he had arrived safely. He tried to remember his e-mail address, but got one digit wrong. The message was received by the widow of a vicar who had died two days before. It read: "Dear wife ... Just checked in. Looking forward to seeing you here tomorrow. It's mighty hot down here!"

A rather impoverished and elderly man was in arrears with his rent and was at his wits' end what to do. In a moment of inspiration he wrote and posted a letter addressed to "God c/o Heaven," and in touching terms explained his plight and his urgent need for £20 to pay off his arrears. The letter was duly opened at the local Post Office, and the workers there were so touched by it that they had a whip-round which produced £15. The cash was put into an envelope and sent to the man's address. A short time after there came a reply, again addressed to "God c/o Heaven." This read, "Thank you for the money, which will be a great help. I know you really sent me £20, but the balance was nicked by those thieving b-----s at the Post Office."

A bank manager's instruction to his staff was never to do anything when on the telephone to customers but refuse requests for credit. One morning he overheard his chief cashier on the telephone and the conversation went like this, "No ... No ... No ... No ... Yes ... No ... No." When he put the phone down the manager said to him, "Why did you say yes to the customer?" "Because he asked me if I was still listening," was the reply.

A customer was refused an overdraft by his bank. This annoyed him very much and proved very inconvenient to him and to his business, so he went along to the bank and asked to see the manager. "We are very sorry, you can't see him," he was told, "He died last Friday." The next day the customer went to the bank again, and got the same reply. On the third day he went again, and the cashier said, "I told you two days ago he died on Friday. Why do you keep coming?" "Oh," the customer replied, "I love to hear you say it."

When the road in the West End used to go through the Marble Arch, a Rolls-Royce and a taxi were both trying to get through the archway. In desperation the driver of the Rolls yelled, "Do you want the whole of the wretched road?" "No," shouted the taxi-driver, "Only the bit you're on."

On a Friday afternoon a man and a very attractive woman walked into Harrods fur department and the woman selected a most beautiful mink stole, in payment for which her companion wrote a cheque to the shop for £30,000. "I am afraid that we can't release the goods to you," said the assistant, "until the cheque is cleared." "Of course," said the man, "that goes without saying." The couple then left. On the following Monday the man returned to the shop and was told that he could not take the stole away as the cheque had bounced. "Oh," he said, "I didn't come to take the stole away. I came to thank you for an absolutely marvellous weekend."

"How did you know that he was a chartered accountant?"
"Well, the information he gave me was 100 per cent accurate and 100 per cent useless."

An actuary is a man who found accountancy too exciting.

A business man was advised by his lawyer to get in accountants to run his business. He did this, and was later asked by a friend how things were going. "Oh!" he said, "the business runs like clockwork. It's being wound up tomorrow."

A man consulted his accountant about his affairs, and asked, "Do you think there will be a wealth tax?" The reply was, "Why should you worry? You're poor!"

It is sometimes said that an economist is someone who, by looking out of the rear window of a car, can tell you where you're going. Or alternatively is someone who knows 250 ways of making love, but doesn't know any women.

Gather two economists together and you will get three opinions.

A consultant is often defined as someone who borrows your watch, tells you the time, and then charges you for the privilege.

Estate agent: "I understand you want to sell your house. May I take a gander round it?" Vendor: "Certainly, if it's house-trained."

An atheist is a man who has no invisible means of support.

A fanatic is a man who redoubles his effort when he has forgotten his aim.

As my old father used to say to me: "We usually get unseasonable weather at this time of year."

Two dogs met in the Park. "My new owners are the tops," said one to the other, "They feed me well, take me for long walks, and tomorrow they're taking me to the vet to be tutored."

In the US deep South, Boudreaux and Thibodeaux are said to be archetypal Cajuns, reputedly rather slow on the uptake. One day Thibodeaux walked along the levee to his friend Boudreaux' farm, knocked on the door, which was open, and got no reply. So in he went, helped himself to beer from the fridge and sat on the balcony to await his friend's return. Towards sunset he noticed Boudreaux in the distance standing in the middle of a field. He made straight towards him and asked him what he was doing. "I'm going to win 2 million bucks," said Boudreaux, "cos I'm going to get a Nobel Prize." "How can that be?" said Thibodeaux, "What you have to do to win that Prize?" "To win that prize," replied Boudreaux, "you have to be out standing in your field."

A gentleman was approached by a friend in Piccadilly wearing clothes which, not to put too fine a point on it, were well below the best sartorial standards. "It doesn't matter how I dress in London," said the gentleman to his friend, "nobody knows me." Not long afterwards the same friend ran into him again in the country. On this occasion his clothes were no better. "It doesn't matter what I wear here," he said, "everybody knows me."

PT Barnum was told of the death of the performer who was fired from a cannon in one of his circuses. He bowed his head and said, "This is grave news. It will not be easy to find a man of the same calibre."

A friend of mine recently escaped from a near fatal experience with a horse. Everything had been fine until the horse started bouncing uncontrollably. He tried to hang on, but was thrown off. With his feet caught in the stirrups and his wife watching helplessly he fell head first to the ground as the horse kicked and thrashed. He was just about to give up all hope of escaping the wild animal when the manager of the supermarket came out and unplugged it.

A man was so worried by what he had read of the dangers of smoking that he gave up reading.

An elegant lady in a first class railway carriage asked the gentleman sitting opposite to her, "Do you mind if I smoke?" He replied, "Madam, do you mind if I am sick?" She rejoined, "Do you realize that I am one of the directors' wives? He replied, "Even if you were his only wife, I should still be sick!"

A friend composed a requiem for the funeral of Rossini. After the funeral he asked another friend what he thought of it. "Well," said his friend, "to be frank, it would have been better if you had died and Rossini had lived."

An old lady attending a concert on the pier while she was on holiday at a well-known seaside resort, listened with rapt attention to a piece of music which the orchestra was playing. At the end she went up to the conductor and said, "Excuse me, may I ask if you could possibly play Boccarini's Minuet?" "Madam," replied the conductor, "that is the piece we just played." "Oh," she replied, "I wish I'd known. It's my favourite." The previous day two elderly ladies who were rather short-sighted and not very with it, had listened to the same piece of music, but could not remember what it was, so during the interval one went to the notice board beside the orchestra, and when she came back she told her friend that it was the Refrain from Smoking.

A young composer had written two pieces of music and asked Rossini to listen to them and say which one he preferred. He was half way through the first when Rossini said, "You need not play any more. I prefer the other one!"

> Between an optimist and a pessimist
> The difference is rather droll,
> The optimist looks at the doughnut
> The pessimist looks at the hole.

How to tell you're growing old:

- everything hurts, and what doesn't hurt, won't work
- you feel like the morning after and you haven't been anywhere
- you finally reach the top of the ladder and you find it's leaning against the wrong wall
- you look forward to a dull evening
- you turn out the lights for economic rather than romantic reasons
- you sit in a rocking chair but can't get it going

- you're 17 round the neck, 42 round the waist, and 106 round the golf course
- the little old lady you help across the road is your wife
- you know all the answers but nobody asks the questions
  and
- you stoop to do up your shoelaces and say to yourself, "is there anything else I can do while I'm down here?"

It is a condition of most motor insurance policies that, within a short time after an accident in respect of which a claim under the policy is to be made, the insured person should write to the insurance company and describe the circumstances of the accident out of which the claim arises. A high standard of literacy is not essential, and most reports of this type are written under a degree of strain or stress. This may account for many which sound to an impartial observer quite bizarre. Among them are the following:

* To avoid a collision I ran into the other car.
* I collided with a stationary tree.
* Accident was due to the road bending.
* Dog on the road applied brakes causing a skid.
* Car had to turn sharper than was necessary owing to an invisible lorry.
* Cow wandered into my car. I was later informed that the cow was half-witted.
* She suddenly saw me, lost her head, and we met.
* A lorry backed through my windscreen into my wife's face.
* I misjudged a lady crossing the street.
* I heard a horn blown and was struck in the back. Evidently a lady was trying to pass me.
* Three women were talking to each other, and when two stepped back and one stepped forward I had to have an accident.
* The accident was due to the other man narrowly missing me.

* I blew my horn but it would not work as it was stolen.
* A lamp-post bumped into my car, damaging it in two places.
* I thought the side window was down, but it was up as I found out when I put my head through it.
* I consider that neither vehicle was to blame but if either was to blame it was the other one.
* One wheel went into the ditch. My foot jumped from the brake to the accelerator pedal, leapt across the road to the other side and jumped into the trunk of a tree.

American visitors planning to visit the UK show a remarkable degree of confusion, to judge by queries received by the British Tourist Authority's New York Office. Typical are the following:

* "Are the Cotswolds open on a Sunday."
* "Do you have running water."
* "What are the ski conditions like in Huddersfield?"
* "Is my Undergroundpass valid to Edinburgh?"
* "Are there any Catholic churches in Dublin?"
* "May I have a list of inns near the mountains and lakes in the East End of London."

Equally amusing are the signs in fractured English so often encountered in our foreign travels.

* "Ladies, leave your clothes here and spend the afternoon having a good time" (Ladies' laundry in Rome).
* "Drop your trousers here for the best results" (Dry cleaners in Bangkok).
* "The lift is being fixed for the next day. During that time we regret that you will be unbearable" (Hotel in Bucharest).
* "To stop the drip turn cock to right" (Finland).
* "Please leave your values at the front desk" (Hotel in Paris).

* "Because of the impropriety of entertaining guests of the opposite sex in the bedroom, it is suggested that the lobby be used for this purpose" (Hotel in Zurich).
* "Ladies are requested not to have children in the bar" (Norway).
* "Not to perambulate the corridor in the hours of repose in the boots of ascension" (Austrian ski resort hotel).
* "Walkings and other starts in bath clothes must be done by the lateral stairs" (Hotel in Iguaçu).

* "When passenger of foot heave in sight, tootle the horn. Trumpet him melodiously at first, but if he still obstacles your passage then tootle him with vigour" (Tokyo car rental firm's brochure).

* "To move the cabin, push button for wishing floor. If the cabin should enter more persons, each one should press a number of wishing floor. Driving is then going alphabetically by national order" (Belgrade Hotel).

Notable graffiti:

"The meek shall inherit the earth - if that's all right with you."
"I am neither for nor against apathy."
"The British are so apathetic - who cares?"
"Be alert - your country needs lerts."
"Due to lack of interest tomorrow has been cancelled."
"Graffiti are dying - the writing is on the wall."

Limericks of doubtful provenance:

There was a young scholar of Johns
Observed to be f*****g the swans
Up rushed a porter
Said, "Sir, take my daughter,
Them swans is reserved for the dons."

There was a young scholar of Trinity
Who ruined his sister's virginity,
B******d his brother,
Had twins by his mother,
And then took a first in divinity.

There was a fine scholar of Kings
Whose mind dwelt on heavenly things
But his mortal desire
Was a boy in the choir
With an **** like a jelly on springs.

There was a young lady of Calais
Who danced the Parisian ballet.
The holes in her drawers,
Drew roars of applause,
For the hairs on her head didn't tally.

Three light-hearted graces

The Lord be praised,
My belly's raised
An inch above the table.
And I'll be damned
If I'm not crammed
As full as I am able.

God of goodness, bless this food
And keep us in a pleasant mood.
Bless the chef and those who serve us,
From indigestion Lord preserve us.

Bless this food, O Lord divine,
Who turnest water into wine,
Forgive O Lord these foolish men
Who try to turn it back again.

Playgirl Incorporated
Centrefold Division
London WCI
Tel: 01-969 3281

Our Ref: SD/am/6059

Your Ref:

Dear ~~Judge Mason~~

Your name has been submitted to us, together with a photograph, but I regret that we will be unable to use your body in our Centrefold Display.

On the scale of 0 to 10 your body was rated -2 by a panel of women judges, whose ages ranged from 62 to 76. We tried to assemble your panel from the age bracket 25 to 35, but unfortunately we were unable to get them to stop laughing long enough to reach a decision.

Should the tastes of British Women change so drastically that bodies such as yours could be used, you will be notified by this office immediately. In the meantime, we have taken the liberty of submitting your photograph to our sister publication, the "Saudi Arabian Camel Keeper", which as you may know is a weekly publication.

Yours with sympathy and sincerety,

Sophie Dunnall

SOPHIE DUNNALL
Editor of Playgirl Incorporated

P.S. We do commend you for your unusual pose. Were you wounded in the war.?

With an acknowledgement to
Stephen Harris